private Screenings

private Screenings

insiders share a century of great movie moments

The American Film Institute
with Duane Byrge
Foreword by James Stewart

Turner Publishing, Inc.
ATLANTA

Library of Congress Cataloging-in-Publication Data

Private screenings: insiders share a century of great movie moments /
    American Film Institute; foreword by Jimmy Stewart. — 1st ed.
        p.   cm.
    ISBN 1-57036-151-7 (alk. paper)
    1. Motion pictures—Anecdotes.   I. American Film Institute.
PN1994.9.P75   1995
791.43—dc20   95-16343
                                                        CIP

Published by Turner Publishing, Inc.
A Subsidiary of Turner Broadcasting System, Inc.
1050 Techwood Drive, N.W.
Atlanta, Georgia 30318

Distributed by Andrews and McMeel
A Universal Press Syndicate Company
4900 Main Street
Kansas City, Missouri 64112

First Edition 10 9 8 7 6 5 4 3 2 1

Editor: Alan Axelrod
Design Director: Michael J. Walsh
Designer: Robert Zides
Production Coordinator: Ellen Bedell
Copy Chief: Lauren Emerson
Picture Editor: Marty Moore
Picture Researchers: Woolsey Ackerman, Lillian Dean,
                    and Kerry Barnett

Printed in the U.S.A.

appearing
(in alphabetical order)

james stewart · foreword

As a movie actor, what you're doing is giving people little tiny pieces of time they never forget. And this is what they remember. Often, it's the movie itself or even a whole scene. They're just short pieces—a look, a reaction, the way you said something.

I know this is true and not just some theoretical notion, because it's happened to me a number of times. People will come up to me and say, "You know, there was this movie you were in, I can't remember its name, but you're in this bar, and you're very depressed, and everything's been going wrong for you, and then you look up and start saying this little prayer. I'll always remember that."

Well, I'm very flattered every time that happens, and I've been lucky enough to have it happen to me more than once. People remember these little moments as vividly as if they were parts of their own lives. It's all connected somehow—their lives and these movie moments.

I know I remember movies that way, too, mostly as short moments. But these moments have had a life-long impact on me. They were often simple, but they all were built along some sort of bigger idea, like in Frank Capra's *Mr. Smith Goes to Washington*, for instance, where the idea was that you were not born

James Stewart, 1935

to be a failure. Or, in *It's a Wonderful Life*, which shows that one man can make a difference. The fact that people remember these tiny moments, when they don't necessarily even remember the name of the picture or the plot, just shows that people remember the abstract idea through the human moment in film. They don't remember it abstractly, they remember it because it had some sort of emotional effect on them.

As I read through the wonderful and touching remembrances in this book, I got a little emotional over many of them. You can see how deeply people are affected by the movies. The many stars from all of the movie fields who contributed to this book have chosen some great scenes. Just reading through them has jarred my memory, given me a few goose bumps and chuckles when they mention scenes that, in just about every case, I can picture in my mind as vividly as if I were sitting in the sixth row, in the dark. In many cases, these remembrances are from childhood, when we're most impressionable. I still remember my first movie-going experiences as a boy back in Indiana, Pennsylvania. We only had one movie theater in Indiana. It would play two bills a week, one on Monday, Tuesday, and Wednesday, and then they'd open a new one. I used to go all the time. I've had a number of wonderful moments in movies, and many of them are from my early growing-up years. There are so many, and I'm just glad they didn't try to pin me down with picking out just one moment and let me do this foreword instead.

A hundred years of film: it's hard to believe the movies have been around that long, but then it's even harder to imagine when they weren't around. ✪

In *It's a Wonderful Life*, 1946

James Stewart
Beverly Hills, California
1995

privateScreenings

glory

debbieAllen

Director, writer, choreographer, and producer Debbie Allen made her debut on Broadway in the chorus of *Puerile*. She went on to appear in *Raisin* and in the 1979 production of *West Side Story*, for which she received the prestigious Drama Desk Award and her first Tony nomination. She later earned two Emmys as choreographer-director for the TV series *Fame* and a Best Actress Golden Globe Award for her role as a dance teacher on the show. Allen received her second Tony nomination for *Sweet Charity* (1986–87) and was the choreographer of the musical *Carrie* with the Royal Shakespeare Company.

In 1988, she took over as director and producer of television's *A Different World*, and that same year, starred in, directed, produced, co-wrote, and choreographed *The Debbie Allen Special*, for which she received two Emmy nominations. Allen received an additional Emmy nomination in 1989 for her work on the muscial *Polly*. In 1992, she directed the TV movie *Stompin' at the Savoy* and for five years has choreographed the Academy Awards show.

Allen has appeared on the big screen in *Jo, Jo Dancer, Your Life Is Calling* and *Ragtime*. In 1995, she returned to television to star in the series *In the House*.

Denzel Washington in *Glory*, 1989

Growing up in the fifties and sixties in Texas, a trip to the movies was always a great treat. It meant popcorn, hot dogs, candy, at least one great cartoon, and at least two star-driven family entertainments like Elvis's *Love Me Tender* or Charlton Heston's *Ben Hur* or Doris Day's *Pillow Talk* or John Wayne's *True Grit*—my dad's favorite—and it only cost fifty cents.

Back then, all of the movie theaters, like the restaurants, amusement parks, and pony rides, were segregated, so, thanks to Jim Crow, there was little expectation of seeing black people in roles that were not domestic, comic, or musical. There was certainly a glimmer of hope with Lena Horne's glamorous musical spectacles, but, invariably, it was more Bill Robinson helping Shirley Temple tap her way to happiness.

The first time I saw black people featured on the big screen as leading characters was in 1959, when my dad took me to see *Porgy and Bess*. Dorothy Dandridge was the most beautiful woman I had ever seen and Sidney Poitier the most love-struck man. My dad told me I could grow up to be like Dorothy Dandridge. In retrospect, the absurdity of "I Got Plenty of Nothin'" at the time of the rise of Dr. King and the Civil Rights movement was all too typical of Hollywood.

When asked to talk about the most meaningful moment I experienced in the movies, I certainly have to recall my father, Dr. Allen, who always took me to the movies, my grandfather Papa Lloyd, a train conductor, and all of the men in my family I considered heroes, who fought for America in Korea and Vietnam, and who fought also to make the world a better place for their families.

There was no moment more relevant than Denzel Washington's performance in Ed Zwick's *Glory*, a movie about the 54th Massachusetts Regiment of black Union soldiers in the Civil War, who struggled for recognition as men and for their identity as Americans. The scene when Denzel is whipped for his apparent desertion (which later turned out to be nothing more than an unauthorized search for a pair of shoes that wouldn't leave his feet blistered and bloodied) captured in a few moments the pain and the suffering African-Americans have endured in an ongoing struggle for human rights. The strength, dignity, and defiance of Denzel Washington's performance gave new meaning to the words *power* and *honor*. It was cinema at its best and so significant in undoing the decades of wrongful images black people have been trying to overcome since *Birth of a Nation*. ✪

Denzel Washington in *Glory*, 1989

picnic

david**Ansen**

David Ansen is a movie critic and senior writer at *Newsweek* and was previously the critic and film editor for *The Real Paper* in Boston. Ansen has served on the selection committee for the New York Film Festival since 1990 and is a member of the National Society of Film Critics and the New York Film Critics Circle.

He wrote the Ace Award–winning TNT documentary, *All About Bette*, profiling Bette Davis, and documentaries on Groucho Marx (for HBO) and Greta Garbo (also for TNT). For several years he was a host of the Bravo Channel's *International Film Festival*.

Sex, love, violence, death—plus music. These are what primal movie memories are all about, and those are the scenes that leap to mind when I free associate on the moments that twisted and nourished my ten- to twelve-year-old soul. I see Rock Hudson in *Giant* in a knock-down, drag-out battle with a bigoted café-owning thug who refuses to serve Hudson's Latino daughter-in-law while "The Yellow Rose of Texas" blasts from the jukebox. And Rock loses the fight! The creepily beautiful underwater image of dead Shelley Winters sitting in her car at the bottom of the river in *The Night of the Hunter*. The shocking, masochistically pleasurable spectacle of William Holden dying in Korea at the end of *The Bridges at Toko-Ri*. Movies could indeed have unhappy endings! That otherworldly, time-shattering kiss between Jimmy Stewart and Kim Novak in *Vertigo* as the camera swirls in a circle around them. Some dim, terrifying recollection of childhood trauma (something under a house; kissing a corpse) that explains why Joanne Woodward went crazy with multiple personalities in *The Three Faces of Eve*. The long, perfect, autumnal last shot of *The Third Man* as Alida Valli walks straight past Joseph Cotten to the throbbing, melancholy zither music of Anton Karas. A sleazy, disturbing B-movie memory of a woman, her clothes ripped, against a tree where she's being assaulted in a forgotten flick called *Portland Exposé*.

Was it a rape scene? Did I even know what that meant? Was real life this mean?

But if I had to single out one indelible sequence—and a famous one it is—it came in 1955 when I went to see the very "adult" movie *Picnic*. There was a hunger up on the screen that stirred something in my ten-year-old being, and it came to a head in that sultry scene of the outdoor dance. Colored paper lanterns hang in the air, and, on the dance floor, tan, love-struck William Holden, his shirt torn from Rosalind Russell's drunken, hysterical lust, approaches Kim Novak, who slides toward him with that sleepy, blurry, touchingly dumb sexuality, swinging her elbows and hips in a slow, insinuating shuffle, while on the soundtrack "Moonglow" plays, and then the strings of the *Picnic* theme soar between the notes.

Now this was hot stuff, and achingly romantic, and though I'm sure I didn't know that I was living in the famously repressed fifties, this steamy summer-night dance pointed the way out of what I wasn't even old enough to be in yet and probably set a romantic standard that real life has been coming up short against ever since. What I do know is that I went back to see the movie a second time and prolonged the mood by rushing out to buy the 45-rpm of the "Moonglow"/*Picnic* theme. Four decades later, it only takes a few notes to transport me back where it all began, and it never ends. ✪

William Holden and Kim Novak in *Picnic*, 1955

14

the gold rush

richard**Attenborough**

Sir Richard Attenborough was born in 1923 and spent his childhood in Cambridge and Leicester. At seventeen, he moved to London for study at the Royal Academy of Dramatic Art, making both his first West End stage appearance and his screen debut in 1942. He has starred in numerous stage plays and almost sixty films, including Steven Spielberg's *Jurassic Park* and John Hughes's *Miracle on 34th Street*. Attenborough became an independent film producer in 1959 and a director in the late sixties. As a filmmaker, he is best known for *Gandhi*, winner of eight Oscars in 1982. In 1971, Attenborough helped establish Capital Radio, Britain's first independent entertainment station, and he was one of the leaders in the creation of Channel 4 Television. Attenborough has headed the Royal Academy of Dramatic Art, the Actors' Charitable Trust, the British Film Institute, and the British Academy of Film and Television Arts. He was knighted in 1976.

In the early 1930s, the journey by steam train from our home in Leicester in middle England to London —a distance of some ninety miles—took little short of two hours. It was considered something of an adventure to undertake the entire trip, there and back, in a single day.

My father and I rose very early on the morning of our eagerly anticipated treat and, on arrival at London's Euston Station, first made our way to the National Gallery and thence to the nearby London Pavilion in good time for the matinee performance of a film made by someone my father described as "a genius." The film was *The Gold Rush*, and the genius, of course, was Charlie Chaplin. My father loved comedy and was totally intrigued by this new medium. I, on the other hand, had hardly ever been to the cinema and had only just heard of Chaplin. I was eleven years old.

The London Pavilion seemed enormous, but when the lights went down and the organ disappeared

Charles Chaplin in *The Gold Rush*, 1925

Olivier said, "perhaps the greatest actor in the cinema," but that, above all, he is a clown.

Shooting on *The Gold Rush* started in the year I was born. Shown in 1925 and, of course, given a new track with Charlie's commentary for its re-release in 1941, it is—depending on how you calculate—either seventy or fifty years old.

There is a current fashion for denigrating Chaplin. "His comedy is crude." "His characters are caricatures." "He is simply not funny." Well, yes, he is in some terms dated. Why wouldn't he be? I wonder, for instance, what we would think of the great Grimaldi these days. But surely no one who truly understands cinema will doubt Charlie's invention or his clowning genius. From *The Gold Rush*, for instance, the tilting cabin scene, the dance of the rolls, and the filleting of the boot all spring instantly to mind.

Charlie himself said that this was the film he wished to be remembered by. But when my mind ranges over his whole body of work, I doubt I could make such a choice. What about *The Kid* or *City Lights* or *The Great Dictator*?

Anyway, for the purposes of these few words, I have singled out *The Gold Rush*, first revealed to me during that London adventure of my boyhood. For, more than any other, it was this magical, unforgettable film, so long ago, which determined that I wished to be an actor and maybe, just maybe, might even one day become involved in the cinema. ✪

into the floor, the atmosphere seemed suddenly to be on a very personal level. I felt a sense of extraordinary excitement, seated in this darkened auditorium and mesmerized by the screen's flickering light, which seemed to be at the end of some vast tunnel.

Father had told me Mr. Chaplin would make me laugh, and laugh I most certainly did. But what I had not expected was the sadness, almost pain at times. And it all happened so rapidly, one emotion almost tumbling over the next. Charlie's virtually unique ability to involve our emotions in what is essentially a comedic context is extraordinary. It is, I suppose, due to the fact that he is not simply a comic and, as

alec**Baldwin**

Alec Baldwin made his professional debut in the NBC daytime soap opera *The Doctors* and later performed in several television programs, most notably the CBS series *Knots Landing* and the NBC miniseries *Dress Gray*. In 1986 he debuted on Broadway in Joe Orton's *Loot* and received the Theatre World Award. He has since appeared on stage in a variety of productions including David Mamet's *A Life in the Theatre*. After starring in a number of films, Baldwin returned to Broadway to appear in *Serious Money* and the 1992 revival of Tennessee Williams's *A Streetcar Named Desire*, for which he received a Tony nomination as Best Actor. Baldwin received an Obie Award in 1991 for his onstage performance in *Prelude to a Kiss*. He later co-starred with Meg Ryan in the film version.

Baldwin has appeared on film in *She's Having a Baby, Beetlejuice, Married to the Mob, Talk Radio, Working Girl, Miami Blues, Great Balls of Fire, The Hunt for Red October, Alice, Glengarry Glenn Ross, Malice, The Getaway*—a remake of the Steve McQueen classic, with co-star and wife Kim Basinger—*The Shadow*, and *Heaven's Prisoners*.

last tango in paris

Watching movies today is considerably different from when I was a child. There was no cable television, pay-per-view, or video rentals. You either went to a theater or you watched movies on broadcast television. The three networks each had a weekly evening movie show, but in New York, "junkies" like myself would be watching *Million Dollar Movie* on WOR-TV or *The Late Show* on CBS.

Before Letterman, CBS broadcast *The Late Show* at 11:30 at night. At 1:30 A.M. it was *The Late, Late Show*, and around 3:15 A.M. it was *The Late, Late, Late Show*. I could have gone even another round. I would sneak down into our living room and watch *How Green Was My Valley; Five Graves to Cairo* (with Franchot Tone and Akim Tamiroff); *Body and Soul; Sorry, Wrong Number; Passage to Marseilles; Beau Geste; A Place in the Sun;* and *Inherit the Wind*. I would stay up until 3 A.M. just to see Elia Kazan's death scene in *City for Conquest* with Cagney and Arthur Kennedy. All gangster films had an infinite entertainment half-life. *Angels with Dirty Faces*, *Dead End*, *White Heat*, and *Little Caesar* were as satisfying the fifth time as they were the first.

There were some inviolable standards in our house. We would read *The New York Times* television guide, which had tiny, clever capsule reviews of the week's movies on television. It was my Bible. In

Maria Schneider and Marlon Brando in *Last Tango in Paris*, 1972

planning my week, any Hitchcock film or movies with Basil Rathbone or Brando were a lock. Biblical epics were big. Gregory Peck was a favorite.

Seeing movies in the theater was a whole other thing. I remember seeing *How the West Was Won*; *It's a Mad, Mad, Mad, Mad World*; *Bye-Bye Birdie*; *The Sound of Music*; and *My Fair Lady* as a child and thinking that movie stars weren't real people. They didn't come from earth but were brought in from another planet.

As I got older, I saw *In Cold Blood*, *Patton*, *The Exorcist*, *M*A*S*H*, *Rosemary's Baby*, *Jaws*, *Serpico*, and *The Godfather*. For the first time, I wondered if they would suspend the extraterrestrial casting requirement in my case. As a child, I loved Julie Andrews, but people like Al Pacino and Robert Blake made me want to be an actor. In 1976, I went to college and visited my first revival movie house. I saw *Last Tango in Paris*, and that changed everything. If Brando had that kind of courage, maybe I could, too. ✪

my fair lady

kim**Basinger**

Born in Athens, Georgia, Kim Basinger was a hometown beauty queen who, upon moving to New York, became a top fashion model before leaving for Hollywood to perform in television movies and miniseries. She made her motion picture debut in 1981 in *Hard Country*, followed by *Mother Lode* with Charlton Heston, and gained widespread attention in the James Bond adventure *Never Say Never Again* (1983). These films were followed by roles in Blake Edwards's *The Man Who Loved Women*, *The Natural*, the controversial *9½ Weeks*, *No Mercy*, and *Blind Date*. In 1989, Basinger created the character of Vicki Vale in *Batman* and starred in *Nadine* and the fantasy *My Stepmother Is an Alien*.

She has also appeared in *Final Analysis*, *Cool World*, *The Real McCoy*, and had a memorable cameo in *Wayne's World 2*. Basinger co-starred with her husband, Alec Baldwin, in the remake of *The Getaway* and starred in Robert Altman's *Ready-to-Wear*.

When I was a little girl, my father took me to the Palace Theater in downtown Athens, Georgia, where they were showing the Russian Ballet Company on film. That's all I remember, just Daddy and me watching those incredible dancers on screen. I don't even know or remember the name of the actual film, but the greatest significance it had in my life was that it symbolized my first real association with "The Movies."

I had been in ballet classes since I was three years old and was strongly attracted to the dedication involved and the magnetism and beauty that ballet seemed to possess. At the same time, I was a renowned tomboy who could not be held captive inside the house as long as light was available from the sky. Playing anything and everything under the street light was a very common activity and took precedence over everything else, but just let someone mention that there was a movie on TV starting at nine o'clock, and I would be the first kid curled up on the floor with my Daddy in front of the television (having finished my nightly bath and teeth-brushing routine). Nothing could keep me from that treasured experience—watching my Daddy's face in the dark with only the light of the TV casting shadows as he watched Jack Lemmon and Lee Remick in *The Days of Wine and Roses,* Steve McQueen in *Baby, the Rain Must Fall,* Gary Cooper and Ingrid Bergman in *For Whom the Bell Tolls,* and Geraldine Page, my all-time favorite actress, in *A Christmas Memory,* just to name a few. It was the ultimate high for me.

I saw the effect movies had on my father and a stirring of emotions in him that I seldom ever saw in real life. It was during those moments I knew exactly where it was I wanted to be. Those bigger-than-life images with their beautiful faces and freedom of expression imitating reality, demanding and receiving all of my father's attention, were probably the main reason I became an actress.

Then came the afternoon of my first date with a boy. A dance was being held at the girls' Y. I had already washed and rolled my hair, sunbathed, and done menial little tasks all day simply to pass the time, but with more than five hours of anticipation left ticking slowly at my being, I decided to go to the movies rather than sit around the house wrestling with the clock. So *My Fair Lady* it was, with Audrey Hepburn. Sitting there in the theater I became so engrossed in the music, the scenery, the characters, their accents and ability to be so believable, that it overwhelmed me with emotion. I sat there crying, not caring who saw me or whether I ever had a date or put on an ol' dress or had anything to do with anything other than my goal, which was to be an actress in the movies.

I was hooked. I love making movies, and I'm truly grateful for all those magical moments in front of the TV as a kid, when the thought of being an actress was just a mere beginning of a wish. Now, I'm simply grateful for the many wonderful experiences I've had between action and cut. ✪

Jeremy Brett, Audrey Hepburn, and Rex Harrison in *My Fair Lady,* 1964

martin**B**rest

Raised in the Bronx and a graduate of the New York University School of the Arts, Martin Brest wrote and directed the short film *Hot Tomorrows* in 1977, while he was a Directing Fellow at The American Film Institute. Brest later wrote and directed the feature film *Going in Style* (1979), starring George Burns, Art Carney, and Lee Strasberg. In 1984 he directed Eddie Murphy in *Beverly Hills Cop*. This film was followed by two movies Brest produced and directed, *Midnight Run* (1988), starring Robert De Niro and Charles Grodin, and *Scent of a Woman* (1992), starring Al Pacino. The latter received Academy Award nominations for Best Picture, Director, Screenplay, and Actor (which Pacino won), and four Golden Globe Award nominations.

My favorite movie scene is the one from Charlie Chaplin's *City Lights*, in which the Flower Girl presses a coin into the Little Tramp's hand, and she realizes that he is the one who gave her the money for the operation that restored her sight. I think the ending is the most glorious moment in movies and, as one film critic once said, "the most rarefied moment in cinema." The whole movie delivers you up to that rarefied level, so overwhelming in its emotion.

The thing you have to remember about *City Lights* is that it is of its time. It's completely different from anything that could be made today. It's almost a fable. Some of its elements could be deemed trite if you judged them by contemporary filmmaking standards. However, it transcends time, and it transcends style. Because it is a fable, children can watch it and enjoy it. Yet, what's truly remarkable is that adults are completely drawn into this story, which, if you tried to describe to somebody, would sound intolerably melodramatic.

I've tried to analyze the plot and character values of that last scene, but that hardly communicates what happens to you when you watch it. Even thinking about the scene brings me to tears. I've seen it over and over for many years, but its power remains undiluted. To savor the scene, you have to backtrack to what leads up to it.

The Chaplin character, the Little Tramp, has fallen in love with the blind Flower Girl. Through a complicated set of circumstances—and one of the film's most beautifully staged sequences—she comes under the impression that her admirer is rich. She surmises that he's probably extraordinarily handsome and dapper, as well. Superficially, she couldn't be more wrong. Yet the inner qualities of the Little Tramp are precisely what she imagines them to be.

The Little Tramp, having fallen in love with her, decides he will make life good for her. He takes a series of horrendous jobs, including one as a boxer. He'll do anything to save this woman. By and by, he learns of a miracle operation—performed only by some doctor off in Switzerland or somewhere—that will restore her sight. In the process of trying to obtain the money for the surgery, and through a wonderfully contrived series of circumstances, he winds up getting his hands on the money legitimately. Yet, through another set of wonderfully designed circumstances, he ends up getting thrown into prison, though not before giving the money to the girl.

He goes to jail. Fade Out.

Fade In: He's released from prison—somehow. He was a tramp going in, but now he's *really* a broken man. He's walking down the street, and we cut to the Flower Girl, who is no longer blind. No longer selling flowers out of a little pail on the street corner, she now has an adorable shop. She has her sight, and her life is just magnificent. She looks out the front door, a big limousine pulls up, and this tall, handsome guy gets out and comes into the store.

Her heart stops. He comes in, looks at her, and she looks at him. He wonders why she's looking at him so strangely. Of course, she still doesn't know who gave her the money for the operation that changed her life.

And we cut to Chaplin as he comes down the street. Kids who remember him from before torment him. They fire at him with a peashooter, and he starts to hobble away—but then he looks down and sees some rose petals on the street, just swept from the woman's flower shop. He bends down to pick up the petals, and the Flower Girl sees him. She says to her mother, why don't we give him a flower and some money? She calls him over. He looks up and sees her. Just stops in his tracks. Not only can she see, she can now see him, see who he is. After the initial joy of seeing what he has done, the Little Tramp wants desperately to get away, because he is so ashamed of himself.

But she runs after him and grabs him. She sticks a flower in his hand, along with a coin. While she's holding his hand, something about his touch makes her realize who he is. She stops dead, too.

This is the moment.

These two people look at each other, the Little Tramp realizing the beautiful thing he did, while she realizes that he was her benefactor. Love is in this moment, yet also tragedy: He's not what she thought; he can't be what she wants. It's an exquisite moment, the two of them looking at each other. It's just unbelievable. I'm getting choked up now recalling it. ✪

Virginia Cherrill and Charles Chaplin in *City Lights*, 1931

lilies of the field

leVar **Burton**

LeVar Burton entered a Catholic Seminary at the age of thirteen to study for the priesthood and left four years later to earn his B. A. at the University of Southern California. Burton landed his first acting job at nineteen, the powerful role of Kunta Kinte in the acclaimed television miniseries *Roots*. The success of *Roots* launched his career, and what followed were starring roles in a string of television movies. Among Burton's feature film credits are *Looking for Mr. Goodbar* and *The Hunter* with Steve McQueen.

In 1983 Burton became the host and co-producer of *Reading Rainbow*, the Emmy-winning PBS children's series, and in 1986 he was cast as Lt. Commander Geordi LaForge in the hit TV show *Star Trek: The Next Generation*. He made his directorial debut with an episode of *Star Trek* and has directed episodes of *Star Trek: Voyager*.

With his partner, Julia Roberson, Burton has founded Eagle Nation Films, a production company.

Sidney Poitier in *Lilies of the Field*, 1963

My favorite movie of all time is *Lilies of the Field*, and it also has my favorite scene, the "Amen" scene at the end of the movie. I think Sidney Poitier's performance as Homer Smith is a large part of the reason I became an actor. I was seven, maybe slightly younger, when I first saw it. I just remember loving Sidney Poitier. I wanted him to be my father. His character of Homer, the handyman, was such an attractive character, really warm. He was his own man, and he had such a great heart.

Homer was really gracious to those German nuns, who wanted to build a chapel. He had such a tremendous depth of feeling and empathy for their dream of building that church. After he had taken on the task to help them, he became determined to build the entire chapel by his own hand. All of the townspeople realized what a daunting task it was and came to him to offer their help. He wanted to do it alone, but they finally wore him down, and he accepted their help. That's also a great scene: we see this man who has so much force of personality, so much character, but we also see the softer side of him, a very inspirational side.

But it is the ending, the "Amen" scene, that is my all-time favorite. It's in the chapel, and Homer is teaching these German nuns, who are fresh off the boat, English. And he teaches them English with a black

26

spiritual. The scene begins as the nuns are singing Gregorian chants, sharing some of the richness of their tradition with him. After they're done, he says, "Let me share with you a little bit of mine." He teaches them the "Amen" song. Once they've learned the parts, he starts them up singing it again and then sort of sneaks out. As he departs, he says to himself, "I done built me a chapel." Then he drives off into the sunset. That was so graceful.

I've probably seen *Lilies of the Field* at least thirty times. It remains at the top of my list because it had such a major impact on my life. My first love was the church, and I actually studied for the priesthood for four years before I decided to become an actor. But when I made that decision, it was because of Sidney. If it hadn't of been for his Academy Award–winning performance in *Lilies of the Field*, the door would not even have been there, let alone open for me, at least in my mind. His presence on the screen made acting a viable career choice for me. ✪

Sidney Poitier in *Lilies of the Field*, 1963

keith Carradine

Born in San Mateo, California, the son of the late John Carradine (veteran actor and father of acting brothers David and Robert), Keith Carradine got the break that launched his career in 1969, when he spent nearly a year in the lead role of Claude in the Broadway musical *Hair*. Soon after returning to Los Angeles in 1970, Carradine landed the role of a young gunslinger in *A Gunfight* with Kirk Douglas and Johnny Cash. He followed this with a role in Robert Altman's *McCabe and Mrs. Miller* and then went on to star in the Altman classics *Thieves Like Us* (1973) and *Nashville* (1975). Carradine's song "I'm Easy," which he performed in the film and for the movie soundtrack, won an Academy Award and a Golden Globe Award for Best Song in a Motion Picture in 1975.

Carradine has starred in a number of other notable films, including a quartet directed by close friend and fellow Altman protégé Alan Rudolph, *Welcome to L.A.*, *Choose Me*, *Trouble in Mind*, and *The Moderns*. Other films include Ridley Scott's *The Duelists*, Louis Malle's *Pretty Baby*, Walter Hill's *The Longriders* and *Southern Comfort*, and the family film *Andre*. He is featured as Buffalo Bill in the film *Wild Bill*, and stars with Darryl Hannah and Moira Kelly in *The Tie That Binds*.

In 1991 Keith Carradine created the role of Will Rogers on Broadway in the smash hit musical *The Will Rogers Follies*. His performance earned him a Tony Award nomination for Best Lead Actor in a Musical.

captains courageous

Spencer Tracy may just be our greatest film actor. He seems incapable of a false moment on screen. And, of all his memorable performances, his portrayal of Manuel, the Portuguese fisherman in *Captains Courageous*, remains particularly vivid in my mind.

I think I was about ten years old the first time I saw Victor Fleming's film of Kipling's story. I knew that my father was in the movie, so I was anxious to watch when it appeared on television. I remember my father proudly listing *Captains Courageous* among the truly great films he'd had the good fortune to be a part of. I sat waiting for his every appearance, only to be quickly taken in by Tracy's wonderfully simple characterization.

Some thirty minutes into the movie, there's a scene that begins with Manuel reclining on deck while he plays and sings along with his hurdy-gurdy. The song he sings has a lilting melody with a whimsical lyric beseeching a little fish not to cry. Soon, Freddie Bartholomew, as the rich and spoiled foundling, comes up from below deck and engages Manuel in a conversation that leads the boy to his first inkling that there's more to life than money and power. He asks Manuel who taught him the song, and Manuel replies that he's making it up as he goes along, that sometimes he's so full of music he can hardly get it out. That moment was a great inspiration to me, as I was already discovering music as a means of emotional release, and I was fascinated by that weird instrument Tracy was playing. Years later, I was walking through Central Park in New York and happened upon a busker playing a hurdy-gurdy. Immediately the image of Tracy as Manuel came to mind, in Harold Rosson's glorious black-and-white photography, playing his hurdy-gurdy on the deck of the schooner *We're Here.* And with that distinctive sound came flooding back those extraordinary sequences of the schooner race, the fishermen hauling in their lines, my father as Long Jack having the hooks cut from his arm, Tracy sinking into the waves, Mickey Rooney ringing the watch bell, Lionel Barrymore casting salty epithets at the rival captain. As the son of an actor and thus a child of the movies, my mind is admittedly filled with images from the films I've grown up with and seen over the last forty-some years, and these memories can be triggered by any number of stimuli. The strongest associations are always emotional, and—for some reason I don't think I can ever fully explain—that scene between Tracy and Bartholomew touched me in a way I've never forgotten. I suppose that is what good movies do. They touch us. *Captains Courageous* remains one of my favorite films, and I eventually found a hurdy-gurdy as well. I can even play it, after a fashion. "Yea ho, little fish, don't cry, don't cry, yea ho, little fish, don't cry, don't cry. . . ." ✪

Spencer Tracy and Freddie Bartholomew in *Captains Courageous,* 1937

my fair lady

rosalind Chao

Actress Rosalind Chao has starred in the feature films *Going Beserk*, *Memoirs of an Invisible Man*, *Thousand Pieces of Gold*, *The Joy Luck Club*, *North*, and, with Warren Beatty and Annette Bening, in *Love Affair*.

She appeared in recurring roles on television's *Star Trek: Deep Space Nine* and *Star Trek: The Next Generation*, as well as in several TV miniseries and episodic shows. Her theater work includes *The Woman Warrior*, *Green Card*, and *Tap Dancer*.

My favorite movie moment is from *My Fair Lady*. It's the first movie I ever went to, and it's one of my first childhood memories. I was a tiny child when I first saw it at the Egyptian Theater in Hollywood. It played for years there, and I went back regularly.

The moment I'm thinking of is when Audrey Hepburn is about to go down the stairway to the ball. She's been transformed from a rough street urchin into this sophisticated young lady. She's just about to come down the stairway, and she's all dressed up in a wonderful gown. It's the first time that Rex Harrison sees her as this magnificent young lady. As she heads down the stairs, the song "I Could Have Danced All Night" swells in the background.

That movie became a near obsession with me. I kept going back to see it. When it came on TV during the holidays, I'd watch it every time. Now when I think about it, I can somewhat understand what attracted me to it. As a child growing up in Orange County, I was the only ethnic in the school. My entire world was white. I had a lot of real insecurities and a certain amount of self-loathing. I felt

like a real outsider, and I really identified with Audrey Hepburn's character, someone who was able to change herself from what she was into someone so magnificent. Now when I look back at the film, I enjoy it more for the subtleties and things I'd missed when watching as a child: how Audrey Hepburn wished she were back where she was before she was changed. Of course, as a child, you see things more simplistically.

While my memories from that movie come from a child's way of looking at things, I also think that they have influenced me in the way I choose roles. I always look for a character who has a major transformation. The character should have some sort of major growth or change. ✪

Audrey Hepburn in *My Fair Lady*, 1964

white mane

marthaCoolidge

Martha Coolidge began her professional film career directing documentaries. Her award-winning films include *Passing Quietly Through*, *More Than a School*, and *Old Fashioned Woman*, a profile of her grandmother that premiered at the New York Film Festival in 1973. Her first feature-length film, *Not a Pretty Picture*, won a Blue Ribbon Award at the American Film Festival and a Gold Ducat at Mannheim.

Coolidge's commercial feature debut was the hit comedy/romance *Valley Girl* in 1982. Her following features included *Real Genius*, the comedy *Joy of Sex*, the mystery-comedy *Plain Clothes*, and *Rambling Rose*, starring Robert Duvall, Laura Dern, and Dianne Ladd. The film earned two Oscar nominations for Best Actress and Best Supporting Actress, as well as three Spirit Awards from Independent Film Project West for Best Director, Best Picture, and Best Supporting Actress. Coolidge went on to direct *Lost in Yonkers*, adapted for the screen by Neil Simon from his Pulitzer Prize–winning play, and *Angie*, starring Geena Davis.

When I was a little girl, my father took me to see *White Mane*, a short French film about a boy who befriends a wild white horse that was evading capture. The boy lived on a marsh with his parents, or perhaps it's his grandparents. The marsh was inhabited by these wild horses—most strikingly, a white one—and these cowboy-like guys on horseback were always trying to capture the horse and tame it. The boy befriends the horse and ends up riding him, which infuriates the cowboys and makes them more determined than ever to capture the horse. As the boy is riding, they set fire to the marshes, trying to box him in, but he rides through the fire and eludes them. They keep chasing him and chasing him, and finally he rides straight out to sea.

It's this closing scene, as the boy rides the horse straight out to sea, that's made such a lasting impression on me. It's incredibly romantic—a fantasy. Although such an escape ultimately means death, it gives you a tremendous exhilaration and feeling of triumph over the evil forces of civilization.

That movie has lived with me for many years, and I finally found a copy of it recently on laser disc. It's a black-and-white movie, on the flip side of *The Red Balloon*. It spoke to me as a child. It said to me that you can be different and that you can still be free. The film actually implies that you have to die if you are different, but I've always felt that one of the reasons I want to make movies is that I want to prove you can be yourself and not have to pay that high a price. ✪

White Mane, 1954

gunga din

tony Curtis

Star of more than a hundred feature films, Tony Curtis has demonstrated his versatility as an actor in such movies as *Some Like It Hot*, *The Boston Strangler*, *Trapeze*, *Spartacus*, *The Great Race*, *The Sweet Smell of Success*, *Houdini*, *The Great Imposter*, *Operation Petticoat*, *Naked in New York*, and *The Defiant Ones*, which earned him a Best Actor Academy Award nomination.

Born Bernard Schwartz in New York, Curtis first gained attention in a Greenwich Village stage production of *Golden Boy* and was quickly offered a contract by Universal Pictures. His screen debut found him dancing with Yvonne de Carlo in *Criss Cross*, and some forty-five years later Curtis has chronicled his remarkable life and career in *Tony Curtis: The Autobiography*.

I saw *Gunga Din* in New York when I was seven or eight years old, and I've seen it countless times since then. There is a scene near the beginning of the picture that never fails to stir me.

The cast was magnificent: Cary Grant, Victor McLaglen, Douglas Fairbanks Jr. It's always been an inspiration. My favorite moment occurs near the beginning of the picture. It's just after this group of thugs has sold the three Scotsmen a phony map, and the men have finally realized it's no good. Cary Grant is holding one of the cheats by the ankles out over his balcony when one of his cohorts comes up and tells him that the map is a phony. Grant wants to know what to do with the guy he's dangling, and his friend says, "Drop him."

The look on Cary Grant's face is priceless. He didn't overplay it. He played the comedy straight, and that's the way you've got to do it. He was really the first leading man type to play comedy. He was wonderful with physical comedy.

I've savored that scene over and over again, as well as others in the film. But it was at that moment, as he dangled the guy out of his window by the ankles, that I knew I wanted to become an actor.

"That's for me," I thought.

Although I've never studied acting, I go to films all the time and study them. Especially when I was start-ing out, I'd study the way Cary Grant played comedy. Later, when I was under contract to Universal after I had come out of the Navy, they asked me what I wanted to do, and I said a Navy comedy with Cary Grant in it. And that is how *Operation Petticoat* came about. I was elated, getting to star with the man who had inspired me to go into the movies. ✪

the lady eve

lauraDern

Laura Dern, daughter of actors Bruce Dern and
Diane Ladd, made her feature film debut as a
troubled pregnant teen in *Teachers* (1984).
Roles in *Mask* (1985), *Smooth Talk* (1985), *Blue
Velvet* (1986), and *Wild at Heart* (1990) followed. In 1991, Dern won widespread critical
acclaim—and a Best Actress Oscar nomination
—for her performance in *Rambling Rose*, co-
starring Ladd, a Best Supporting Actress nominee.
The nominations marked the first time a mother and
daughter were so recognized in the same year
for the same film.

Dern has also starred in Steven Spielberg's
Jurassic Park (1993) and Clint Eastwood's *A
Perfect World* (1993), and
she has worked on stage
and TV, winning a Golden
Globe for her performance
in the HBO docudrama
Afterburn (1992).

i love movies so much that anytime I've ever been
asked what my favorite movie moment is I have to
say there are about twenty, but I particularly love a
moment from *The Lady Eve*. It's one of my favorite
movies of all time. I love Barbara Stanwyck, and I
love the scene where she is looking through her
make-up mirror at all these women throwing themselves at Henry Fonda.

I first saw *The Lady Eve* when I was about seventeen. I just loved the wit, the charm, the romance,
and the idealism that movies had then. It's so beautifully shot, so clever, and with such wonderful dialogue. I've always loved Preston Sturges comedies. It
was fantastic. I just don't know why it's harder to
make those kinds of movies now. I guess things were
just different then, a little more idealistic and pure—
certainly more innocent, like the screwball romances
where the guy still needs approval from his family to

marry the girl, even though he's about thirty-five years old. He's still asking Mom and Dad for permission to marry the girl, and he's still probably a virgin.

I love that whole period of movie making. I love Howard Hawks's movies, and I feel the same way about Frank Capra's *Meet John Doe, Mr. Deeds Goes to Town, Mr. Smith Goes to Washington,* and *It's a Wonderful Life.* They all showed such a sense of belief in people and a belief in dreams. ✪

Henry Fonda and Barbara Stanwyck in *The Lady Eve,* 1941

little caesar

richardDonner

Director and producer Richard Donner is the creative force behind some of the most popular movies of the last twenty years, including *The Omen, Superman, Free Willy,* the *Lethal Weapon* series, and *Maverick*. His career began in front of the camera, as an actor in Martin Ritt's television production of W. Somerset Maugham's *Of Human Bondage*. "Marty told me I'd never make it as an actor because I couldn't take direction," recalls Donner, "but he thought I could give it, so he offered me a job as his assistant." Donner moved on to direct such television series as *Wanted: Dead or Alive* starring Steve McQueen, *The Twilight Zone, The Fugitive, The Man from U.N.C.L.E.,* and *Kojak*. In 1975 he directed his first major feature, *The Omen,* followed by *Superman: The Movie, Inside Moves, The Toy, Ladyhawke,* and *The Goonies*.

In *Lethal Weapon,* Donner introduced two cops, played by Danny Glover and Mel Gibson, who would become one of the cinema's most popular crime-fighting duos. Donner also produced and directed *Scrooged* and *Radio Flyer,* served as executive producer of *Free Willy* (I and II), and directed and produced *Maverick,* starring Mel Gibson, Jodie Foster, and James Garner.

The most memorable movie moment in my life—and I remember it only as vividly as a mind of that age could—happened when I was four or five years old. It set in motion my entire life.

My grandfather owned a movie theater in Brooklyn, both an outdoor and indoor theater. My parents left me with my grandparents one day, and my grandfather put me in the back row of the theater, right on the aisle. It was my first motion picture, Edward G. Robinson in *Little Caesar*. In fact, my grandfather used to play *Little Caesar* on and off for six or seven years at that time—something my mother later told me.

So there I was, sitting there in a theater all by myself, in the back, at the end of the row. I had never seen anything on a big screen before, nor had I ever heard that level of sound before. That whole experience infected me, and I do call it an infection. Since that day I've been addicted to the movies. As a four- or five-year-old kid, I became hooked on the movies.

The movie moment itself was not particularly noteworthy. It was a car careening around a corner on a dark and rainy night, seemingly coming right at me. It was a big, black, shiny, gangster-type car, and I don't really even remember what happened after that—if it crashed into a pole, or if there was gunfire. It just transfixed me: the combination of the car coming right at me on the big screen and the tremendous sound of the screeching of the brakes.

Maybe, that's why I've done a lot of pictures with all these crazy car chases in them. Sitting there all alone as a little kid on the end of the back row with this great big black car coming right at me. It made a lifelong impression. ✪

38

Edward G. Robinson in *Little Caesar*, 1931

kirk**Douglas**

Born Issur Danielovitch, December 1916, in Amsterdam, New York, Kirk Douglas won a scholarship from the American Academy of Dramatic Arts that put him on the road to Broadway, where he made his debut in *Spring Again*. His performance on Broadway in *The Wind Is Ninety* caught Hollywood's attention, and he was cast opposite Barbara Stanwyck in *The Strange Love of Martha Ivers*.

Three years later, in 1949, his role in *Champion* won him both stardom and an Academy Award nomination. Douglas received his second nomination in 1952 for his performance in *The Bad and the Beautiful*, and his third in 1956 for his portrayal of Vincent Van Gogh in *Lust for Life*.

Douglas broke the notorious Hollywood blacklist in 1958 when his independent film company, Bryna, gave screen credit to blacklisted writer Dalton Trumbo for *Spartacus*. Star of some eighty feature films, Douglas has also acted in several television projects, receiving two Emmy Awards and a Golden Globe nomination. His autobiography, *The Ragman's Son*, was published in 1988, and was followed by three novels.

Douglas has been honored with the Medal of Freedom, America's highest civilian award, and by an appointment as Officier de la Légion d'Honneur for distinguished services to France in arts and letters. He was chosen by The American Film Institute for its prestigious Life Achievement Award.

a moment with dalton trumbo

As I look back and realize that I have made more than eighty movies, it frightens me. It frightens me even more when I realize I can only find about twenty-two movies that I'm really proud of. Fifty-eight clunkers is a lot. But nobody sets out to make a bad movie. Movie making is a collaborative effort and depends on so many elements coming together in the right way to succeed. It's amazing how often those elements fail.

I am reminded of a montage of scenes in *The Bad and the Beautiful*: the camera races through the casting of a movie, the filming of a movie, the editing of a movie, the rushing of the cans of film to a theater for a sneak preview, the anxious producer walking up and down, and the audience rushing out of the theater to fill out preview cards as the camera comes in on a close-up of one of those cards as the patron is seen writing, "It stinks." That's the tragedy that awaits anyone who makes a movie or book, or produces any piece of art that depends on the approval of the public. He risks falling on his ass— a memorable moment, all right, one you'd wish you could forget.

But, thank God, my most memorable moment is one I don't want to forget. It happened during the filming of *Spartacus*. This was a film fraught with problems: injuries to stars, changing of directors, budget overruns. But what a talented cast! This was the first time I worked with Laurence Olivier, a great actor, a gentleman, and a generous teacher who was willing to help you, but only if you asked. How exciting it was to stand on the sidelines and watch Charles Laughton and Peter Ustinov dueling verbally —two champions toying with each other the way a matador toys with a bull. Working with Jean Simmons was a delight, although the love scenes were difficult to do on the screen with all the obstacles placed in our path by the camera, the lights, the crew. And it wasn't easy convincing her to play a scene nude, in the river sequence—unheard of at that time. It was fascinating to watch the genius of a director like Stanley Kubrick at work. He eliminated all the dialogue between Spartacus and Varinia in the mess hall sequence and created a beautiful love scene by the way he let the camera slowly approach, so that the touching of their hands became a moment of great love.

Towering over all these memories, however, is the face of screenwriter Dalton Trumbo.

At that time, Dalton was blacklisted for being a Communist. That, of course, didn't stop studio heads from using his talent, as long as he worked in hiding, and they could pretend someone else had written the script. He had written *The Brave One* as Robert Rich, and when it won an Oscar, Dalton Trumbo could not go up there and get it.

The hypocrisy enraged me, but at first I went along with it. When I hired Dalton Trumbo to write *Spartacus,* I called him Sam Jackson. But one day something snapped. That was the day I wrote out a pass for the screenwriter to come onto the Universal lot. And when I filled in the name, I wrote not Sam Jackson, but Dalton Trumbo.

I'll never forget it. Dalton came to my office, visibly moved. He said, "Kirk, this is the first time I've been allowed on a lot in ten years. Thanks for giving me my name back."

That moment—Dalton Trumbo standing in front of me with tears in his eyes—is my most memorable moment in the movies.

Incidentally, Dalton Trumbo's real name appeared in the film credits. Columnists, critics, and studio heads were enraged. But it was too late. The blacklist was broken and with it ended a period of hypocrisy that existed for much too long and made each one of us in the film industry a little lesser because of it. ✪

unforgiven

billDuke

Director/actor/writer Bill Duke has worked on stage as well as in film and television. As an actor, he has appeared in the films *American Gigolo, Predator, Commando, Bird on a Wire,* and *Action Jackson.* Duke made his feature directorial debut with *A Rage in Harlem,* starring Forest Whitaker, Gregory Hines, Danny Glover, and Robin Givens, and in 1994 directed *Sister Act 2: Back in the Habit,* starring Whoopi Goldberg. He has also filmed *The Cemetery Club,* with Ellen Burstyn, Diane Ladd, Olympia Dukakis, and Danny Aiello, and *Deep Cover,* starring Laurence Fishburne and Jeff Goldblum.

My favorite moment is from *Unforgiven* with Clint Eastwood. It's the scene where Eastwood is talking with a young man who is toying with his gun and is about to go into town. He's practicing his draw, bragging about how he's going to kill somebody.

Eastwood, the old-time gunslinger, is lying there in his bunk with his hat over his eyes, but he's watching the boy fire away. Eastwood says very quietly, "You've got to be careful when you talk about killing a man, because you're not only taking his life, you're taking all that he was and all he's gonna be."

It was one of the most profound film moments I've ever seen. It was the contrast between a guy who had been through it all and a guy who was planning to go through with it, killing a man. The kid had the ego. Death, to him, was something he couldn't conceive. Young and inexperienced, he couldn't understand the importance of another man's life. Metaphorically, the moment also dealt with violence in America and the perception of it as glamorous. In that one moment, Eastwood said a hell of a lot about violence. Although it was very simple, it was very eloquent. It was a western, but its message is contemporary. It is so succinct. It's right there. ✪

43

Clint Eastwood in *Unforgiven,* 1992

the ox-bow incident

clint**Eastwood**

Clint Eastwood began in television, co-starring in the long-running *Rawhide* series as cowboy Rowdy Yates. But it was his move to Italy and his portrayal of the legendary "Man With No Name" in *A Fistful of Dollars*, *For a Few Dollars More*, and *The Good, the Bad, and the Ugly* that fused his image with that of the lone gunfighter.

In 1968, Eastwood formed his Malpaso Company, allowing him to produce and direct as well as star in his own projects. His debut as a director was the chilling *Play Misty for Me*. *Dirty Harry*, directed by Don Siegel, followed in 1970 and created a new screen persona for Eastwood. Hits such as *Joe Kidd*, *High Plains Drifter*, *Magnum Force*, *Thunderbolt and Lightfoot*, *The Outlaw Josey Wales*, *The Enforcer*, *The Gauntlet*, *Every Which Way but Loose*, *Sudden Impact*, *Tightrope*, and *Pale Rider* continued to broaden his appeal. *Unforgiven* (1993) earned Eastwood Academy Awards for both Best Picture and Best Director. Eastwood next starred in the suspense thriller *In the Line of Fire* and directed and starred opposite Kevin Costner in *A Perfect World* and Meryl Streep in *The Bridges of Madison County*.

Henry Fonda, Dana Andrews, and others in *The Ox-Bow Incident*, 1943

A number of moments come to mind, but there are a couple from *The Ox-Bow Incident* that stand out for me. There's a very difficult moment in the film when Henry Fonda has to read a letter from the guy (Dana Andrews) who is killed. The way the director William Wellman staged that was unique. He showed us the reactions on everybody's faces as Fonda was reading the letter. It was very powerful to do it that way. You saw it all: the hurt and shame in their faces. You didn't need a lot of dialogue.

There's also another very emotional moment from the movie that has made a lasting impression on me. It's an action moment when Fonda tries to intercede in a mob. It wasn't just a fightfight. It was more like people just mauling each other. The fighting didn't seem organized. It seemed very real. It didn't have the typical, staged Western fight look, where people throw punches and miss, falling down all over the place. It was one of the great mob moments. You felt that here was a group of people out of control. It seemed very real and very frightening. That's a moment that's always indelibly stuck in my mind.

I first saw the movie in the mid-1940s, when it came out, and I was very impressed with it. I rented it recently, and it seemed to hold up. It's one of those movies that you just need to sit there and be with, like *Sunset Boulevard* or *Double Indemnity*, great films that you've just got to hang in there with from the beginning to end because they're all these very powerful moments within them. ✪

the third man

rogerEbert

The only motion picture critic to have won the Pulitzer Prize for distinguished criticism (1975), Roger Ebert has been the movie reviewer for the *Chicago Sun-Times* since 1967. His reviews are distributed to more than two hundred other newspapers around the country and are available in book form in the annual editions of *Roger Ebert's Video Companion*. Ebert is also the author of *A Kiss Is Still a Kiss* (1984); *The Perfect London Walk* (1986) with Daniel Curley; *Two Weeks in the Midday Sun* (1987), a journal of the Cannes Film Festival illustrated with many of Ebert's own drawings; *The Future of the Movies* (1991) with Gene Siskel; and *Behind the Phantom's Mask* (1993), a humorous whodunit. Since 1976, Ebert and the *Chicago Tribune's* Gene Siskel have reviewed movies together on national television.

Orson Welles in *The Third Man*, 1949

A rainy August day in Paris, the summer after my sophomore year in college. Unseasonably cold. I had never been in Europe before, spoke no French, knew nothing about Paris I hadn't learned from *Arthur Frommer's Europe on $5 a Day*. I was somewhere on the Left Bank, wrapped in a raincoat, my feet squashing through puddles. The poster outside the movie theater showed Orson Welles, Joseph Cotten, Trevor Howard, and Alida Valli. *The Third Man*. *L'homme troisième*. I had heard the theme song by Anton Karas, on the zither, a hundred times. I had never seen the movie. I paid a few francs and entered the darkness of the little repertory house, a smoky cave that smelled of sweat and Gauloise cigarettes. The rows were so close together that the seat in front cut into my knees.

I never knew the old Vienna, before the war . . . Scenes of the partition of the city. . . . A man named Lime.

Every seat was filled. I became conscious of the reverent attention of the audience; they took this seriously, in a way that the movie audiences of my

experience had not taken movies. This was more than a screening; it was an attendance at the greatness of the film.

The towering shadow of the balloon-man against the wall. The way Valli's hands, in Lime's apartment, betrayed how well she knew it. The exact tilt of the shot in which Cotten signals to the flower vendor in the nightclub. The evil little man with his observant little dog. Trevor Howard, as a man who has seen it all and is bemused by the naiveté of his American visitor. The round-faced little boy, leading the chase. The cat rubbing against the shoes in the doorway. And then Orson Welles, in the most famous entrance in the history of the movies, smiling teasingly across a wet street, before a car rushes past and he disappears.

If there was a moment at which I understood what the movies were, and could be, it happened while I watched *The Third Man* that afternoon in Paris. I was touched on every level it is possible for a movie to touch me. I loved the romance, the cynicism, the sadness, the bravado of the visual style, the harsh detachment of the music, the interplay between Welles and Cotten on the Ferris wheel, and most of all the resigned poetry of the final shot, with Valli walking out of Cotten's life, and then the way he lit his cigarette and wearily threw away the match. ✪

Orson Welles in *The Third Man*, 1949

indiscreet

nora**Ephron**

Nora Ephron began writing for the movies after years as one of the country's best-known journalists. Starting as a newspaper reporter for the *New York Post*, she became a magazine writer for *Esquire*, the *New York Times Magazine*, and *New York* magazine, among others. After taking her talents to the big screen, Ephron has received Best Original Screenplay Academy Award nominations for *Sleepless in Seattle*, *When Harry Met Sally*, and *Silkwood* (co-written with Alice Arlen). Her other screenwriting credits include *Heartburn*, adapted from her bestselling novel of the same name, *Cookie* (also co-written with Arlen), and *My Blue Heaven*.

Ephron turned to directing in 1992 with her first feature, *This Is My Life* (for which she also wrote the script). She followed it in 1993 by directing Meg Ryan and Tom Hanks in *Sleepless* and, later, Steve Martin in *Mixed Nuts*, co-written with her sister Delia Ephron.

Cary Grant and Ingrid Bergman in *Indiscreet*, 1958

I have many favorite movie moments, and almost all of them are directed by Stanley Donen, but there is one particular moment that stands out in my mind. It's from *Indiscreet*. The scene is a split screen, with Cary Grant on one side and Ingrid Bergman on the other. They're talking on the telephone to each other

50

from their respective hotel rooms. Both of them are lying down on their beds as they talk. As they're talking, Ingrid Bergman moves her hand in one direction from her head, and she says, "We are good for each other." As she moves her hand and says that line, he squirms on his bed, as if she's touched him. And he says, "We are, we are."

It put me away when I first saw it. It still does. It's divine. I looked at that scene again before we did our split screens on *When Harry Met Sally*. It was, to me, the quintessential, romantic split-screen moment between a man and a woman. I just loved it. Stanley Donen, forever and ever. ✪

a moment with james cagney

milos**Forman**

After making several films in his homeland, Czech director Milos Forman came to Hollywood in 1968. His first American film, *Taking Off* (1971), was chosen as the official U.S. entry at that year's Cannes Film Festival, where it took the Jury Prize. He contributed to *Visions of Eight* (1973), in which eight directors explored the Munich Olympics, and afterward directed a Broadway play. Forman's next movie was *One Flew Over the Cuckoo's Nest* (1975), which won Oscars for Best Picture, Best Director, Best Screenplay, Best Actor (Jack Nicholson), and Best Actress (Louise Fletcher)—the first time a film had received all five major awards since *It Happened One Night*, forty-one years earlier.

Forman also directed and co-wrote the 1979 movie musical *Hair*. He then filmed *Ragtime* (1981) and *Amadeus* (1984), which swept the Academy Awards with eight Oscars, including Best Picture, Best Director, Best Screenplay Adaptation, and Best Actor (F. Murray Abraham). This triumph was followed by *Valmont* in 1989.

James Cagney had already been confined to a wheelchair and was a recluse, but for the benefit of financially needy old actors he accepted an invitation to appear in the *Night of 100 Stars*, a big charity extravaganza in New York's Radio City Music Hall.

We were ushered into a large space, three flights below the ground, from where, during the regular shows, the entire orchestra was ceremoniously lifted directly onto the stage on a huge, moving platform. The idea was that James would be raised up on the stage for the finale. Once up there, all the other stars would surround him for the evening's climax.

So we were sitting in this spacious cavern: James, his wife, Willy, and their friends Marge and Don Zimmerman, waiting for the big moment.

On the TV monitor, we watched what was happening onstage. One star after another appeared before the packed house. To thunderous applause, they sang their songs, told some anecdotes, or simply saluted the evening and its noble purpose.

And every time the likes of Bette Davis, James Stewart, Cary Grant or other old-timers would

appear on the monitor, James's shoulders would begin to shudder, and silent tears would roll down his cheeks, as if somebody had told him that this night was going to be the last time he would be with his friends on the same stage.

We were sitting there, respecting an old man's melancholy. Nobody said a word. Then suddenly Marge pointed to the monitor in disbelief.

"This is the finale! James, the finale is on! They forgot about you!"

It *was* the finale. They *had* forgotten about James Cagney!

I began to sweat, and Marge started to cry.

In that moment, James took his eyes away from the monitor for the first time. He looked at us, a big smile illuminated his face, and with a shrug, he said gently: "That's showbiz!"

And he laughed. ✪

James Cagney, 1931

the deer hunter

jodie Foster

Jodie Foster is an accomplished actress and director, whose performances in *The Accused* (1988) and *The Silence of the Lambs* (1991) earned her two Academy Awards for Best Actress. She was again Oscar nominated for *Nell* (1994) and received a Best Actress Golden Globe Award for her work in the film, the first project produced by her own production company, Egg Pictures. In 1991, Foster made her motion picture directorial debut with *Little Man Tate*, in which she also starred, and she has directed and produced *Home for the Holidays*, starring Holly Hunter and Anne Bancroft, for Egg.

Foster began her career at age three and made her feature debut in *Napoleon and Samantha* when she was eight years old. She received her first Oscar nomination for Martin Scorsese's *Taxi Driver* (1976).

With time off from her career to attend Yale University, Foster has appeared in more than thirty-two films, including *Alice Doesn't Live Here Anymore* (1975), *Bugsy Malone* (1976), *Little Girl Who Lives Down the Lane* (1976), *Freaky Friday* (1977), *The Hotel New Hampshire* (1984), *Stealing Home* (1988), Woody Allen's *Shadows and Fog* (1991), *Sommersby* (1993), and *Maverick* (1994).

Movies were my family's own personal obsession. Some of my earliest memories take place in drive-ins, art houses, specialty film bookstores. Very often, my mother would pick us up from school and head directly to a double feature. If it was good, we'd always see the movie more than once; if it was awful, we'd walk out. Because I was a child actor, analyzing the merits and flaws became a very serious task, one that the whole family could take part in. But it wasn't until I had twelve or so films under my belt, an Oscar nomination, and countless hours logged in the flickering dark that I finally had my perfect movie moment. The film was *The Deer Hunter*. The scene was about Russian roulette. Robert De Niro and Christopher Walken have been captured by the Viet Cong. After a few days of torture and abuse, they are forced to submit to a death game by their screaming, drunken captors. These two friends since birth must pass a loaded pistol

53

across to one another and pull the trigger (as their captors yell and slap them in the face), all the while looking into each other's eyes. I remember feeling so intimate with the De Niro/Walken characters that I experienced the fear and pain behind their faces. I was inside them, looking out. I was experiencing the desperate, primordial urge to live, the painful urge to die, the shame of their humiliation, the awful and

beautiful connection between them that no one would ever understand, a thousand different human emotions in a sea of terrible chaos. And there I was, fourteen years old, weeping uncontrollably in some movie theater with an hour to go yet. This scene happens in the second act, and the rest of the movie is informed by the experience. So even as the soldiers return home to a surreal American embrace, you can't shake the Russian roulette scene. You just keep welling up long after the movie is over, well into the ride home. If I think really hard right this minute, I can feel it again. It's as if some unconscious memory comes flooding in, some collective experience that finds its voice in that scene. In my own work, I keep looking for that, that tissue of connection that is as undeniable as it is unexplained, that piece of humanity. You can't analyze it. You just live it. Moments like that turn a film buff into a life buff. I keep hoping that's the point. ✪

Christopher Walken in *The Deer Hunter,* 1978

state fair

john**Frankenheimer**

John Frankenheimer's films, from *Birdman of Alcatraz* and *The Fixer* to *Seven Days in May*, *The Manchurian Candidate*, and *Year of the Gun*, tackle important social and philosophical topics. He started his career in television, directing weather and news shows, then moved up to the classic *Playhouse 90* anthology series. He turned to the big screen in 1956 with the theatrical version of his television drama, *The Young Stranger*. His next film was *The Young Savages*, followed by *Birdman of Alcatraz* and *All Fall Down*, one of only three U.S. entries in the Cannes Film Festival of 1962. That same year *The Manchurian Candidate* was released, and over the next few years, Frankenheimer's films included *Seven Days in May*, *The Train*, *Grand Prix*, *The Fixer*, *Seconds*, *The Gypsy Moths*, *The Horseman*, *The Iceman Cometh*, *French Connection II*, *Black Sunday*, and *52 Pick Up*.

W

When I was about thirteen I saw the movie *State Fair*, and I saw Jeanne Crain and that long hair just bouncing up and down as she walked across the screen, when she was walking away from her first date with Dana Andrews back to the family trailer. That made more of a lasting impression on me than anything I'd ever seen on film. I saw that movie fourteen times. I even remember where I saw it; it was at the Taft Theatre in Flushing, Queens.

I fell wildly in love with Jeanne Crain. I read about her. I bought movie magazines to read more about her, and I was absolutely devastated when she got married to someone. After that I guess I probably started going to more movies, but this remained my key movie. ✪

Dana Andrews and Jeanne Crain in *State Fair*, 1962

all about eve

william**Friedkin**

William Friedkin began his career in the mail-room at WGN-TV, Chicago, and within two years was directing live television. In the space of eight years he directed more than 2,000 live programs. His first work in film was *The People vs. Paul Crump*, a documentary about a man who spent eight years on death row in the Cook County Jail, which earned Friedkin the Golden Gate Prize at the San Francisco Film Festival and resulted in the commutation of Crump's sentence. Friedkin went on to make such documentaries as *The Thin Blue Line, Mayhem on a Sunday Afternoon,* and *The Bold Men.*

His first feature film, *Good Times* (1968), was followed by *The Night They Raided Minsky's* (1968), *The Birthday Party* (1969), *The Boys in the Band* (1970), and *The French Connection* (1971), which won him a Best Director Oscar and was voted Best Picture. Next came *The Exorcist* (1973), *Sorcerer* (1977), *The Brinks Job* (1979), *Cruising* (1981), *Deal of the Century* (1983), and *To Live and Die in L.A.* (1985). In 1986 Friedkin returned to television, then directed *Blue Chips* (1994) for Paramount Pictures.

George Sanders and Anne Baxter in *All About Eve*, 1950

My most memorable movie moment is a scene from *All About Eve*, which is one of my five favorite films. It's a scene just before the finale of the film, between George Sanders, who plays a theater critic named Addison DeWitt, and Anne Baxter, who plays a young actress named Eve Harrington. She's the protégé of an older actress played by Bette Davis.

Eve is in her hotel room, about to go onstage before what turns out to be her award-winning performance. Addison DeWitt comes up to her hotel room, and he unmasks her as a complete fraud. It's one of the most beautifully orchestrated scenes I know of, starting with the writing. Also, the simplicity of the way it was filmed and edited makes the intensity all the stronger. It is really a classic piece of American screenwriting and direction, both done by Joseph Mankiewicz. His dialogue is incredible.

The scene not only sums up the plot, but unveils the characters as well, encapsulating the power struggle between the two leads. It is kind of a classic male/female power scene, brilliantly performed and written.

I first saw it many years ago in a Chicago movie theater and was initially very impressed by it. Over the years, I've seen it probably twenty-five more times, and I've come to realize how brilliant it is. It just gets richer and deeper for me. ✪

ashes and diamonds

scott Glenn

Scott Glenn began acting as a way of becoming a better writer. A newspaper reporter, he studied acting to learn the realities of dialogue for a planned novel. Small parts in such films as Robert Altman's *Nashville* and larger parts in some of Roger Corman's low-budget movies followed, but it was Glenn's starring role with John Travolta and Debra Winger in *Urban Cowboy* that launched his career. Next came performances in *The Right Stuff*, *Silverado*, *Personal Best*, *Apocalypse Now*, *The Challenge*, *Backdraft*, *The Hunt for Red October*, *Silence of the Lambs*, *My Heroes Have Always Been Cowboys*, *Tall Tales*, *Flight of the Dove*, and *Night of the Running Man*.

A lifetime member of The Actors Studio and a student of Lee Strasburg, William Hickey, and George Morrison, Glenn has performed in off-Broadway productions and Lanford Wilson's Broadway play *Burn This*.

Zbigniew Cybulski in *Ashes and Diamonds*, 1958

For me, the last scene in the movie *Ashes and Diamonds* by Andrzej Wajda is visually stunning. The actor Zbigniew Cybulski dies in a garbage heap at the end of the film. The image stands so strongly in my mind because it is one of what I consider the three perfect film performances. Marlon Brando in *Last Tango in Paris* and Dexter Gordon in *'Round Midnight* are the other two.

It was the way Cybulski drew his character. He played someone who had spent most of World War II as a teenager living in the sewers. Now his eyes couldn't handle any light, so he wears dark glasses all the time. Here's a guy who knows nothing but fighting in some sort of literal underground movement. Now he's maybe twenty-three or twenty-four years old. The war is over, so there are no Nazis left to fight, but now his group has turned right wing, and the enemy is the Polish Communists.

But Cybulski's performance is less political than personal. That he can make this character delicate, poignant, and moving is remarkable. All of the work Cybulski does in the film and the way Wajda shoots it contribute to those qualities. The whole opening section, for instance, where two young guys are just lying in the sun in the shade of a church. They're talking to each other, and you don't know what it's about. It feels just like two guys lying under the sun. And then they roll off their backs, and what is underneath are submachine guns. They're going to assassinate the new Communist official.

That whole film stands in my mind for those two images: of Cybulski dying in a garbage heap and of those two young assassins lying in the shade of a church. ✪

danny **Glover**

in the heat of the night

One of Hollywood's most versatile and respected actors, Danny Glover has gained international star status for his portrayal of police detective Roger Murtaugh opposite Mel Gibson in the mega-hit *Lethal Weapon* series of films.

The actor's early film credits include *Escape from Alcatraz* and *Chu Chu and the Philly Flash*, followed by *Iceman*. In 1984, Glover received widespread acclaim for his portrayal of Moze in the Academy Award–winning *Places in the Heart*.

In 1985, Glover starred in three films of tremendous range: *Witness*, *Silverado*, and *The Color Purple*.

Glover was inducted into the Black Filmmakers Hall of Fame in 1990 and also received the prestigious Phoenix Award from the Black American Cinema Society. In 1991 he starred in *Flight of the Intruder* and *A Rage in Harlem*, and he co-starred in *Pure Luck* and *Grand Canyon*. *The Saint of Fort Washington* and the powerful drama *Bopha!*, based on the life stories of children of black South African police, followed in 1993. Glover also starred in the live-action baseball comedy-fantasy *Angels in the Outfield* in 1994 and made his directorial debut in 1995 on Showtime with the Chanticleer Films production of *Override*.

Sidney Poitier and Rod Steiger in
In the Heat of the Night, 1967

There's a moment between Rod Steiger and Sidney Poitier in *In the Heat of the Night* that's very special to me. It's when Steiger says, "What do they call you? Virge? Virgil? Virgie?" And Poitier replies, "They call me *Mister* Tibbs."

Every time I see that scene, it sends a chill through me. The way in which Sidney says it, the way in which he defines himself is so amazing: "They call me *Mister* Tibbs." He says it with such incredible humanity and dignity. I'll always remember that.

I first saw the film when it came out. I was about twenty. Because of the times and my being black, it was a golden, rich moment for me. Sidney's always provided us with rich, unforgettable moments. There are certain people you revere. You always remember them.

I see *In the Heat of the Night* occasionally now on TV. When I saw it last, it did the same thing to me. It's still very vivid for me, still affects me the same way it did the first time I saw it. That shows you the power of movies and how they transcend time. You can always call on that moment, the richness of that moment. It can still elicit from you something that is really human. It lives on. ✪

Laurence Olivier and Merle
Oberon in *Wuthering Heights*,
1939

wuthering heights

lee **G**rant

Lee Grant made her stage debut at the age of four in *L'Orocolo* at the Metropolitan Opera in New York. She studied at the Neighborhood Playhouse School of Theatre and, while still in her teens, won the Critics Circle Award for her Broadway performance in *Detective Story*. Her role in the film version of the play earned her the Cannes Film Festival Citation as Best Actress and her first Academy Award nomination.

Immediately after this impressive screen debut, she became a victim of the McCarthy era blacklists. By 1966, Grant had resumed her career with *Peyton Place*, for which she won an Emmy Award. She went on to win a second Emmy for *The Neon Ceiling*, an Oscar for *Shampoo*, and Academy Award nominations for *The Landlord* and *Voyage of the Damned*.

Grant began her directing career in 1989 with the feature film *Staying Together*. Her HBO documentary *Women on Trial: America Undercover* received a 1994 Cable ACE Award nomination, and her *Down and Out in America* won an Academy Award in 1987 for Best Documentary.

There has been a kind of unfolding series of memory moments, personal revelations, that have had an impact on each different period of my life through film. When I was a child I saw *Wuthering Heights*. I was a voracious reader of Brontë and Austen and the Russian novels, too. *Wuthering Heights* set the mold for passion and undying love in my mind. I fell in love with Heathcliff—it may have set my life pattern. I've always been attracted to men who were outsiders, volatile, who were not considered "proper."

The next real revelation, still from childhood, was when the RKO Hamilton on 145th Street in Manhattan had a retrospective of French films. I saw *The Baker's Wife* and *Grand Illusion*. It had never occurred to me there was a different kind of reality. It was like all those Cartier-Bresson photographs of working people. There was no glorification of the beautiful, wealthy people who were on our screens at the time. French directors showed working people; they were tough. And the leading lady wasn't beautiful; she was real, and she still got the guy.

After that, *The Bicycle Thief* and Anna Magnani's pictures were great influences. Those postwar Vittorio DeSica films were revelations. Again, the characters were real people, not celluloid images. Next was Costa-Gavras's *Z*. That was staggering to me. Seeing that, I think, had a lot to do with my making documentaries. Add Altman and Bergman—all of these filmmakers opened my mind to new worlds and gave me a fresh look into my own. I don't think I've lost my fascination with the romance of Heathcliff, but each of these other films has added to my reality and changed the direction in which I was going. ✪

muriel

randa**Haines**

Randa Haines made her motion picture directorial debut with *Children of a Lesser God*, which was nominated for five Academy Awards, including Best Picture, and Haines was nominated for her work by the Directors Guild of America. After *Children of a Lesser God*, she filmed *The Doctor*, starring William Hurt, Elizabeth Perkins, and Christine Lahti, and directed Richard Harris, Robert Duvall, and Shirley MacLaine in *Wrestling Ernest Hemingway*.

Haines studied acting with Lee Strasberg and appeared off-off Broadway. After gaining initial film production experience at a small company where she did everything from buying the props to editing sound effects, she became a script supervisor for almost ten years. In 1975 she was accepted into the Directing Workshop for Women at The American Film Institute in Los Angeles. There, she co-wrote and directed *August/September*, based on part of a novel by Doris Lessing. The impressive result led to her work as a writer for the highly respected television series *Family* and then as director of numerous television specials and series episodes.

Delphine Seyrig in *Muriel*, 1963

My great movie moment is not a great moment in movies particularly, but it was a great moment for me personally. When I was living in New York, pursuing acting—I was between eighteen and twenty-two—I used to go just about every day to the Museum of Modern Art to see the movies that they showed. This was during the time they were showing all of the Godard films, that whole incredible New Wave of amazing movies.

They showed *Muriel* by Alain Resnais. I had come out of a childhood of a lot of isolation and loss. At the time, I was struggling to figure out who I was. I had been on my own since I was eighteen, since the day I finished high school. I went to see *Muriel*, which starred Delphine Seyrig, an incredible actress. She was playing a woman who was an antiques dealer and whose apartment was her shop. People would come to her place and see antiques in a homey environment. Consequently, everything she lived with was for sale; there were price tags hanging on everything. Her character seemed to be a woman who carried so much sadness, was such a tragic heroine. I remember she had such an incredible style about her. I remember her clothes and the way she wore her hat. She had all this amazing furniture. And the way she cooked, everything had such style.

The film deals with a lot of missed opportunities and past misunderstandings: "Why weren't you in the cafe at ten o'clock twenty years ago?"

"But I was there. I was sitting behind the palm."

I remember sitting there watching the movie, and I think I felt that way about my own life. At the time, I felt sadness and loss, like a tragic heroine in my own story. I remember sitting there thinking, "Well, if I'm going to be a tragic heroine, I should try and do it with that sort of style." And then I thought, "Wait a minute. Why should I be a tragic heroine at all?"

Her character looked like she might just dissolve at any moment. A lot of her energy just went into holding herself together. I think that was the way I felt. It was her presence and her character and everything that surrounded it—that sense of the missed opportunities of the past.

I remember there's one character that sings a song to her, someone from her past. It's an incredibly sad song called "Déjà," which means "already." The lyrics were about the twenty years that had already passed. She sang that a capella to Delphine Seyrig in a cafe. It was aching. The whole time Seyrig was just holding herself together, fighting the feeling that any moment she might just dissolve with the pain she is carrying. I identified with that, rather than just with the particulars of the story. I identified with the quality of that character and all that surrounded her.

I determined that this type of character wasn't who I wanted to be. I didn't want to be a tragic heroine. Why should I have to see myself that way? I have fought that feeling all my life. That movie was a real turning point for me.

Also during that same period I saw Godard's *Masculine-Feminine*, where the character played by Jean-Pierre Leaud and his girlfriend, played by Chantal Goya, go to see a movie. They are sitting in the theater, watching a strange film. It appears to be a Swedish film, in which the people never say anything, but they kind of grunt in what sounded like Swedish grunting. It's a scene between a man and a woman. She is wearing a slip, getting ready for bed. There is a very unhappy feeling in the air between these two people. It is an awkward moment to witness within two people's lives, in the movie-within-a-movie. As Jean-Pierre Leaud and Chantal Goya are watching the film, a voice-over says, "It's not the movie that each of us carry in our hearts."

When you sit down in a dark theater, it is always with the hope that what you see will be that unknown movie that you carry in your heart, that movie you want to see more than anything in life, a movie that will speak to you.

That has always stuck with me, as a moviegoer and as a movie maker. You want to make a movie that people will carry in their hearts. ✪

2001: a space odyssey

tom**Hanks**

Tom Hanks got his first big break when he was cast in the television comedy series *Bosom Buddies*. He subsequently starred in several motion pictures, including Ron Howard's *Splash* and *Nothing in Common*, *Dragnet*, *The Bonfire of the Vanities*, *A League of Their Own*, and *Punchline*. *Big* earned him his first Academy Award nomination in 1988, and in 1993, Hanks received a Golden Globe nomination for *Sleepless in Seattle*.

His compelling performance as an AIDS-stricken lawyer in Jonathan Demme's *Philadelphia* earned Hanks the 1994 Best Actor Academy Award, and his portrayal of the title role in *Forrest Gump* garnered him a second Oscar the following year. Hanks followed these critically acclaimed performances with a role in Howard's *Apollo 13*.

Without a question, my favorite movie moment is the opening credits as *Thus Spake Zarathustra* plays in *2001: A Space Odyssey*. That piece of music lasts a minute and 56 seconds, and it is choreographed brilliantly against the titles: "MGM Presents A Stanley Kubrick film of Arthur Clark's *2001: A Space Odyssey*."

I first saw it at the Cinerama Dome theater in Oakland when they still gave you a hard ticket, not one off a machine. You got a hard ticket, and they tore it in half. The movie was on the big curved screen. A very big theater. There's something about those domes that have great acoustics. It looked almost like a planetarium. It was clean, and it had that movie-theater smell. I remember going in—you'd have to fan in either to the right or left, and then go up the ramps a long way, deep into the sides of the theater. There was no middle aisle, just stalls, like in England. So, you'd walk forty seats in and sit down. I sat right in the middle.

I was a big space fanatic. I was a planetarium rat, because the Oakland Public School System literally had a planetarium in my neighborhood. I knew a lot of the stars and all about space. I remember I could not sleep the night before I saw the film. I read *The Making of 2001: A Space Odyssey* before I saw the movie.

I saw it on a Saturday afternoon. When the theater lights go down in the afternoon, it is different than when they go down at night, because you've been outside where it's bright. So, it seems even darker in the daytime. When the curtain came up, the first thing I heard was the low-level "whaaaa." That's the best I can explain it. The "whaaaaaaaaaaa" goes on for a very long time. Then it stops, then the first beat of the music comes in.

What Kubrick did visually was to set up the conjunction of the earth, moon, and sun, which plays itself out in the course of the movie. As you are watching, you are behind the moon. It's absolutely dark and the moon suddenly drifts down, and you realize you're on the far side of the moon. There is the earth, and it comes down. Behind it is the sun. The first time the kettle drums thump "Boom, boom, boom, boom," the credits start coming up, all perfectly choreographed. As the fanfare culminates with the brass, those three tones—"Dah, Dah,

Daaaah"—that's when the title *2001: A Space Odyssey* comes right up there.

I don't know what my face looked like when I saw it, but I think it was one big, goofy grin. I don't think there's a better moment that I've ever had at the movies. To be twelve years old, to be sitting there in that great planetarium-style theater and feeling like you were not just in space, but were seeing things from the other side of the moon—that was amazing.

What is truly amazing is that all this was done with 1968 technology. Kubrick and Douglass Trumbull literally wrote the special effects book with *2001*. I have it on laser disc and every now and again, I just pull that thing out. I still get that big, goofy grin. ✪

2001: A Space Odyssey, 1968

don't look now

renny **Harlin**

Filmmaker Renny Harlin's initial success came with the independent film *Nightmare on Elm Street IV: The Dream Master*. He went on to direct the 1990 smash *Die Hard 2: Die Harder* and made his debut as a producer with the critically acclaimed *Rambling Rose*, starring Robert Duvall, Laura Dern, and Dianne Ladd. In 1993, Harlin produced and directed *Cliffhanger*, and he produced the 1994 romantic comedy *Speechless*, starring wife Geena Davis, Michael Keaton, and Christopher Reeve. He has also directed and produced the pirate epic *Cutthroat Island*, starring Davis and Matthew Modine, and formed, with Davis, the production and development company, Forge.

Several movies and a number of unique movie moments continue to influence my work and life, but one specific sequence has had an impact on me beyond any other cinematic experience.

I was fourteen in 1973 and in Helsinki, Finland, when a blood-red velvet seat in the Gloria Cinema carried me into the eerie and claustrophobic world of Nicolas Roeg's *Don't Look Now*. The entire film threw my pubescent visual imagination into a tailspin. The use of slow motion and the selection of camera angles; the colors of the film, or the lack of them. The integration of sound effects and music. These elements, combined with the bizarre story and realistic characters, formed a chilling, fascinating, and arousing cinematic journey.

The culmination of these ingredients is the lovemaking scene between Julie Christie and Donald Sutherland. Sex scenes in general are notoriously hard to shoot. In most films they seem unnecessary and gratuitous. We've seen everything from slow motion to spinning cameras and smoky rooms with venetian blind-filtered light. We've seen graphic, and we've seen subtle. We've seen grabbing, sucking, and licking, but year after year this love scene remains way beyond anything that the imitators can come up with.

It is very realistic, even graphic, but at the same time extremely warm and caring in the portrayal of this husband/wife relationship. The scene is brilliantly intercut with images of both of them getting ready for an evening out. As they dress and groom themselves for the outside world, we see them simultaneously peel off all the layers of pretension to reach the kind of intimacy only real love can give you. What also makes this scene so memorable is its juxtaposition against the wintry cold of Venice. It's the only warm and safe haven in the midst of a frightening landscape. As such, it dramatizes the story's core conflict. The struggle of the life force, which is love, with all its naked beauty and vulnerability, in the face of the cold reality of death.

Stylistically, the scene exemplifies the movie's unique representation of reality. Its extraordinary manipulation of images gives the viewer a strikingly vivid sense of the richness and complexity of the experience of being alive.

I will never forget this sequence, and no love scene in another movie could ever be its equal. I remember the theater; I'll never forget that night at the movies. I even remember vividly the young couple sitting in front of me, necking, as the movie went on. I was alone in the theater, not knowing yet how much these haunting images would affect my future. ✪

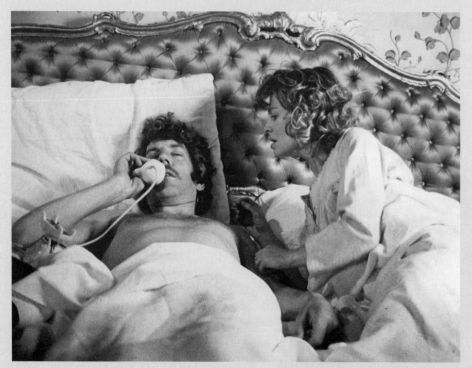

Donald Sutherland and Julie Christie in *Don't Look Now*, 1973

marshall**H**erskovitz
& edward**Z**wick

it's a wonderful life

It was at The American Film Institute, where they were both Directing Fellows, that Marshall Herskovitz met his future partner, Edward Zwick. Herskovitz spent several years writing and directing for episodic televison, including such shows as *Family* and *The White Shadow*, before he teamed up with Zwick to create the multi-award–winning television movie *Special Bulletin*. In 1987, Herskovitz and Zwick collaborated on the television series *thirtysomething*, another multi-award winner. In 1992 Herskovitz directed Danny DeVito in *Jack the Bear*. Later, he and Zwick executive produced the television series *My So-Called Life*.

Zwick began his feature-film directing career with *About Last Night . . .* He went on to direct the Academy Award–winning film *Glory*, as well as *Leaving Normal* and *Legends of the Fall*, which Herskovitz produced.

Herskovitz and Zwick have created The Bedford Falls Company and The Bedford Falls Group—named for the town in *It's a Wonderful Life*—as homes for their film, television, and commercial projects.

We named our company Bedford Falls after the town in *It's a Wonderful Life*—having fallen in love with Capra's film twenty years earlier, before it became a holiday staple. Marshall discovered it one night while still in college, staying up till 3:30 in the morning, unable to turn off this amazing dark poem of modern life.

There is a scene in the film so perfect and so powerful, yet so confounding, that we've talked about it ever since.

George Bailey has come to Mary Hatch's house an unwilling suitor, they've argued, he's left but forgotten his hat; he returns just as Sam Wainwright calls from New York.

"Hee haw," says Mary Hatch, with exaggerated warmth to make George jealous. And their dance of seduction begins.

George squirms, standing so close to this woman who loves him, his own unwanted desire mounting.

"Put him on the extension," says Sam, when Mary reveals that George is there. To which Mary replies, more to George than to Sam, "We can't. Mother's on the extension."

What a moment, as we cut to the mother upstairs—busted. Mary didn't even have to look. She knew her mother would be on the extension; her mother's *always* on the extension. This is the work of the master directors—Capra, Cukor, Hawks: unexpected, even eccentric behavior presented off-handedly, thrown away, so funny in its casualness, so convincing in its depiction of the richness and complexity of life. There are so many incredible throwaways in this film: Annie giving money at the end—"I've been saving this money for a dee-vorce, in case I ever got married . . ."

The scene continues, Sam painting the bright future of plastics, George and Mary forced to stand even closer, to hear through the one earpiece. George is smelling her hair, almost unable to contain himself; she is straining upward, toward every possible touch. They're losing track of Sam's pitch; he's asking if George can hear. Mary looks at George, "He says it's the chance of a lifetime . . ."

And then it happens. Not what you would find in any other movie, not what you would find if Capra were really the corny sentimentalist people say he was. They don't start kissing. He starts to shake her instead. Violently.

"Now you listen to me—I don't want any plastics, and I don't want any ground floors, and . . ." He runs out of words. She is crying soundlessly, helplessly—completely open to him, beautiful beyond words. And then he does kiss her, all over her face, holding her as fiercely as he was just shaking her.

And the scene, in all its electric passion, is over, defying all theory.

The modern language of acting speaks of intention and obstacle. The actor must enter a scene with a strong, unshakable action to play. The action is then opposed by an obstacle, and the resulting conflict is the scene. But real life is so often not like that. Our ambivalence is such that we don't always know which is the action and which is the obstacle. And so it is with George in the scene.

What does he really want? To go off and see the world, and leave Mary behind? If so, then his love for her is merely an obstacle—hardly possible when we see how intensely he holds her in the end. But the opposite can't be true, either. If his action is to love her, and the obstacle is his desire to see the world, why does he shake her so violently? That's as powerful as his kissing her two seconds later.

The truth is he wants both in the scene. He's in torment because he has two equal and opposing motivations. How many actors could play that, or even understand the concept? How many filmmakers would be brave enough to try to realize it?

Love, hate, jealousy, sensuality, violence, humor, tears—not bad for three minutes of screen time. ✪

Donna Reed and James Stewart
in *It's a Wonderful Life*, 1946

citizen kane

charlton Heston

Born in Evanston, Illinois, Charlton Heston spent his early years in St. Helen, Michigan, a north-woods hamlet of one hundred residents where his father was a mill operator. Living in an isolated house, "Chuck" learned to amuse himself by acting out the stories his father read to him. When the family moved to Wilmette, Illinois, Heston took full advantage of New Trier High School's excellent drama program, then enrolled in Northwestern University's School of Speech on an acting scholarship.

Heston made his Broadway debut in the cast of Katharine Cornell's 1948 *Antony and Cleopatra*. He first drew Hollywood's attention after playing Antony in David Bradley's widely acclaimed 16mm version of *Julius Caesar*. When producer Hal Wallis saw the picture, he brought Heston to California to play the lead in *Dark City*. Immediately thereafter, Cecil B. DeMille signed him for *The Greatest Show on Earth*, which won the Academy Award for Best Picture. Heston himself won an Academy Award for Best Actor for his performance in *Ben Hur* in 1959 and went on to become one of Hollywood's greatest leading men, starring in nearly sixty feature films.

Joseph Cotten and Everett Sloane in *Citizen Kane*, 1941

For me, it's *Citizen Kane*.

I saw the film when it was first released, when I was studying acting at Northwestern University along with the girl I'm still married to. It knocked us out.

The scene I remember best, the sequence I remember best, is the review of the opera, when Joe Cotten, Kane's friend and his newpaper's drama critic, had to steel himself to write a bad notice about Kane's wife.

He wrote the notice.

I was far too green in my knowledge of film techniques, which at that point was just about zero, to appreciate the groundbreaking quality of the editing and camerawork, things like that. The only thing I could judge with any competence was the acting. And Joe Cotten's performance was great, as great as Welles's, which was probably one of the best performances Orson ever gave on film. But to see how all that worked from the perspective of a young acting student was a knock-out for both Lydia and me. Back then, serious drama students were very snobby and snotty about film. To see a film like this, where a director/actor came from the stage and made one of the great movies of our time, was a marvelous revelation. To see the quality of the acting was just extraordinary.

I've seen better performances, but I'm not certain I've seen a better single film. That whole experience was a sort of Saint Paul on the Road to Damascus thing for me. It opened my eyes to the possibilities of film. ✪

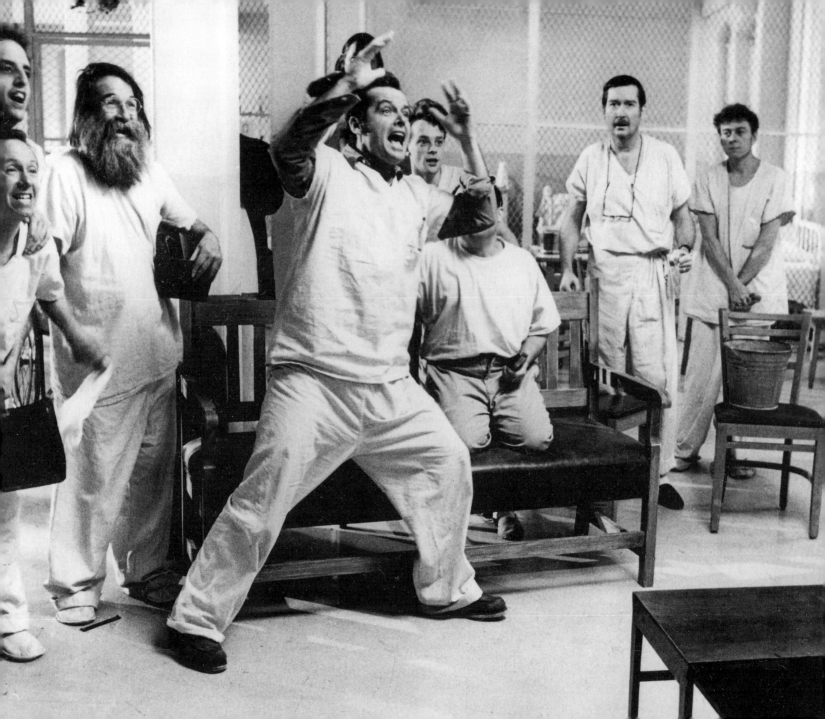

one flew over the cuckoo's nest

ron**Howard**

Born in Duncan, Oklahoma, Ron Howard had his first acting role at the age of eighteen months in a Baltimore production of *The Seven Year Itch*. At the age of four, he made his first screen appearance in *The Journey*. Howard subsequently appeared in *The Music Man* and as Opie in the long-running TV series *The Andy Griffith Show*. In the 1970s, he starred in *Happy Days* and drew favorable reviews in the feature films *American Graffiti* and *The Shootist*.

In 1978, when he was twenty-three years old, Howard directed his first movie, *Grand Theft Auto*. A string of popular hits followed—*Night Shift*, *Splash*, *Cocoon*, *Gung Ho*, and *Willow*—and Howard founded the independent production company, Imagine Films Entertainment, with Brian Gazer in 1986. For it, he directed *Parenthood*, *Backdraft* (which received four Academy Award nominations), *Far and Away*, *The Paper*, and *Apollo 13*.

Jack Nicholson in *One Flew Over the Cuckoo's Nest*, 1975

The scene that sticks with me is the sequence in *One Flew Over the Cuckoo's Nest*, when the patients want to see the World Series, and Nurse Ratchett (Louise Fletcher) won't let them. Jack Nicholson, livid, argues with her, tries to reason with her. But she holds her ground in a very parental, patronizing way.

He suddenly ignites all the patients by simply willing the World Series into existence through the power of his imagination. I remember everybody slowly gathering around him and catching on to what he is doing: creating this very eccentric play-by-play. He describes Sandy Koufax striking out Mickey Mantle, saying, "Koufax's curveball is breaking like a fucking firecracker" and all sorts of stuff like that.

Everybody cheers.

The scene was a turning point in the movie, alerting Nurse Ratchett to the galvanizing power of this amazing character. He asked his fellow inmates to use their imaginations to escape within themselves, and yet also to really share something. He created the mental environment that made this possible. It's a great moment for me. ✪

2001: a space odyssey

gale anne **Hurd**

Producer Gale Anne Hurd has carved her niche in the male-dominated action-adventure genre with such influential and innovative hits as *Aliens, The Terminator, The Abyss, Alien Nation,* and *Terminator 2: Judgment Day.* She began her career at New World Pictures as executive assistant to Roger Corman. Hurd subsequently served as director of advertising and publicity for the company, moved into production as a co-producer, then formed her own company, Pacific Western Productions, which made its debut with *The Terminator,* followed in 1986 by the release of the Oscar-winning *Aliens.*

Pacific Western next produced *Alien Nation* (the basis for the critically acclaimed Fox television series) and the underwater thriller *The Abyss.* In 1991, Hurd executive produced *Terminator 2,* which received seven Academy Award nominations and won four Oscars. 1992 saw the release of *Raising Cain,* written and directed by Brian De Palma.

Hurd also formed No Frills Films, a production and development company specializing in low and moderately budgeted features. In recognition of her commitment to bringing new talent to the filmmaking forefront, The American Film Institute has created the Gale Anne Hurd Production Grants for the Institute's Directing Workshop For Women.

There is a transitional sequence in Stanley Kubrick's *2001: A Space Odyssey* in which primates first learn to use bones as tools and weapons. One bone is tossed into the air, end over end. The next image we see is that of spacecraft in a match-cut from the spinning bone, accompanied by Strauss's *Thus Spake Zarathustra* on the soundtrack. *2001* unequivocally demonstrated to me that science-fiction films could achieve new levels of sophistication in content as well as production values.

I was attending Stanford University when I saw the film for the first time. In fact, I wrote my thesis in film criticism on Kubrick's classic. The year was 1976, and I never imagined that a career in film would become my destiny, nor could I have predicted that I would find my niche in the science-fiction genre. ✪

apocalypse now

david henry Hwang

David Henry Hwang is best known as the author of *M. Butterfly*, which premiered on Broadway and won the 1988 Tony, Drama Desk, and Outer Critics Circle Awards, as well as the 1991 L.A. Drama Critics Award. A film version was released in 1993, starring Jeremy Irons and John Lone.

Hwang's dozen other produced plays include *FOB* (1981 OBIE Award), *The Dance & The Railroad* (1982 Drama Desk nomination; *CINE* Golden Eagle Award), and *Family Devotions* (1982 Drama Desk nomination), as well as the libretto for Philip Glass's opera *The Voyage*. Hwang scripted the 1994 feature film *Golden Gate*, and the 1996 feature *The Alienist*, based on Caleb Carr's best-selling novel.

Martin Sheen in *Apocalypse Now*, 1979

In a sense, I owe my very existence to the movies. As a child growing up in Shanghai, China, my father fell under the spell of American films. Watching *It's a Wonderful Life* and the early MGM musicals gave him a mythical vision of America—a great, boundless land of magical lives and dreams fulfilled. Shortly after immigrating to this country, he met my mother at a University of Southern California foreign students' dance. And so I, the offspring of these dreams, was born an American. Growing up in a different era of films, I, too, found the movies reflecting my personal and political journeys. The features of my youth redefined that American myth spun during my father's childhood. *The Godfather* series re-investigated the American Dream, unearthing the conflict, compromises, and ambivalence beneath an immigrant success story. *Taxi Driver* confronted head-on the violence and moral ambiguity of our national psyche, while *Apocalypse Now* held special significance for me as a story of cultures clashing in confusion, sparking an inevitable spiral into madness and destruction. As I write this, America is proceeding through yet another of those reinventions that so define this dynamic nation. With minorities poised to constitute a majority population within the next few decades, American movies, through independent filmmakers and the increasing awareness of Hollywood studios, continue to explore the emotions and conflicts of our age. From *Do the Right Thing* to *The Joy Luck Club* to *La Bamba* and beyond, today's artists are spinning a new generation of American myths. And my father, and myself, along with millions of others around the world, continue to sit in the dark and watch and dream. ✪

the education of sonny carson

george Jackson

George Jackson's production career began as a production assistant at Paramount Television, where he worked on the sitcom *The New Odd Couple*. He later moved to Universal Pictures, becoming the executive assistant to the president of Worldwide Production. Jackson served as executive vice president of production for Richard Pryor's production company, Indigo, at Columbia Pictures, and became involved in the early career development of many new African-American filmmakers, including Robert Townsend, Reggie Hudlin, and Roy Campanella, Jr. The Harvard University graduate also headed the Griot Entertainment Group, a Warner Bros. partnership that included Quincy Jones, among others. During this period, Jackson, in association with Doug McHenry, developed many projects, including the live stage play *Beauty Shop* and the TV program *Livin' Large*.

Jackson, in association with McHenry, has also produced the feature films *Krush Groove*, *Disorderlies*, *Stalingrad*, *New Jack City*, *House Party II*, and *Jason's Lyric*.

Rony Clanton in *The Education of Sonny Carson*, 1974

The Education of Sonny Carson came out in 1974 and was based on the life of a man who grew up in the slums of Brooklyn. It was all about the days of gang warfare in the inner city during the '50s and '60s, when things were actually much more benign than nowadays: There was a code of honor, and there were no guns. It was just about fists. The particular scene that I'll never forget is when Preacher is preaching at a funeral, and the theme of the sermon is "Who killed Little Boy?" It is riveting. The Preacher indicts all of society for the death of this young man. The performance was so stirring, wonderful, and very powerful in a real way, I questioned whether or not this was a real funeral—perhaps filmed while making the movie. It was an extraordinary piece of acting by an actor I didn't even know at the time. I remember last summer when I went to see the world premiere of *Boyz N the Hood*, and one of the kids is killed in the movie, and his family is all around crying. It brought me back twenty years to when I was a teenager watching *The Education of Sonny Carson*. It saddened me, of course, because the themes were very similar, but it also gave me a great sense of empowerment, because I realized that African-American filmmakers were making movies in a tradition that hasn't really been recognized yet. For instance, when you hear about our films from the '70s, they're referred to as products of the "Blaxploitation Era." Certainly, *The Education of Sonny Carson* was not an exploitation movie. It was the *Boyz N the Hood* of that era. ✪

samuel l. Jackson

Samuel L. Jackson made an indelible mark in film with his portrayal of hit man "Jules" in Quentin Tarantino's acclaimed *Pulp Fiction*. He received a Best Supporting Actor Academy Award nomination as well as a Golden Globe nomination for his performance. His searing portrayal of a crack addict in Spike Lee's *Jungle Fever* won the first and only Best Supporting Performance Award ever given by the judges at the Cannes Film Festival. He also won the New York Film Critics Award for Best Supporting Actor for this performance.

Jackson made his film debut in *Together for Days* and went on to appear in *Ragtime*, *Do the Right Thing*, *Goodfellas*, *Losing Isaiah*, *Kiss of Death*, and *Die Hard with a Vengeance*, among other films. His versatile career also includes television and stage work, originating the roles in two of August Wilson's plays at Yale Rep and earning Cable ACE and Golden Globe nominations for his performance in John Frankenheimer's Emmy Award–winning *Against the Wall*.

Ursula Andress and Peter Sellers in
What's New, Pussycat?, 1965

My discovery of Peter Sellers in *What's New, Pussycat?* turned me on to a whole new world of film. I saw it when I was in high school, when it first came out. I was trying to go see a James Bond movie, but the Bond movie was sold out. I was determined to go to the movies that day, and right next door was *What's New, Pussycat?* I had no idea what it was about, but I didn't want to go back home. I paid my money and went in.

It was the most amazing thing I had ever seen. I had never seen anybody be that silly and that moving at the same time. Peter Sellers played a psychiatrist, and there were all these crazy characters in it. The scene that really blew me away was when Peter Sellers was trying to seduce one of his patients, and his wife, who was an opera singer, stormed in. She was wearing a helmet and a breastplate. I laughed so hard. I had never had that much fun in a movie. I'd never realized, outside of the Three Stooges, that there were movies this funny that actually had a plot. I started seeking out Peter Sellers films, watching for this very disturbed but totally brilliant man. He became one of my favorite actors. ✪

norman**Jewison**

Director and producer Norman Jewison has been a vibrant force in the motion picture industry for three decades. Personally nominated for four Oscars, his films have received 45 nominations and 12 Academy Awards. Jewison made his professional debut on the stage at age five. In 1958, he accepted an invitation from CBS TV to direct *Your Hit Parade*, *The Andy Williams Show*, and various specials, collecting three Emmy Awards in the process.

Jewison's debut as a feature film director came with the 1962 comedy *Forty Pounds of Trouble*, starring Tony Curtis. After *The Thrill of It All*, *Send Me No Flowers*, and *The Art of Love*, Jewison became an independent filmmaker, a move that brought success with his first effort, co-writing and directing *The Cincinnati Kid*. Since then, Jewison has filmed *The Russians Are Coming, The Russians Are Coming*; *The Thomas Crown Affair*; *In the Heat of the Night* (five Academy Awards, including Best Picture of 1967); as well as *. . . And Justice for All*. He also directed the screen version of *Fiddler on the Roof*, the rock opera *Jesus Christ Superstar*, *Rollerball*, and *F.I.S.T.* In 1984 he directed *A Soldier's Story*, adapted from Charles Fuller's Pulitzer Prize–winning play. *Agnes of God* (1985) was honored with three Oscar nominations. His *Moonstruck* (1987) was another multiple Oscar-winner. In 1988 he produced *The January Man* and the next year directed *In Country*. Jewison also directed *Other People's Money* (1991) and *Only You* (1994).

In 1986, Jewison established the Canadian Center for Advanced Film Studies (CCAFS).

keystone kops

I remember when I was extremely young and growing up in the East End of Toronto during the 1930s, I was given a tiny, hand-cranked projector. Such toys weren't very expensive, and I used to put up a sheet, and we used to have shows down in our basement.

I fell in love with what was available, which were the silents. As a result, I became a big Mack Sennett fan, because you could get all of those things: Sennett, Laurel and Hardy, Buck Jones, Felix the Cat, and all the silent cowboy films.

When I was growing up, of course, I had no idea I would become a film director. When I was eight or nine, I used to go to a movie theater in Toronto called The Beach. It cost ten cents for the Saturday matinee. You saw two movies, plus a serial and a cartoon. So you were in the theater from two o'clock until five-thirty, and then you would go home.

I grew up in the Depression, and there wasn't any money. So I would *tell* the film to a group of kids, and they would give me a penny. That way I could go to the movies, and I could tell movies. I would tell the film from beginning to end, acting out all the parts. I went to all sorts of movies, everything from *Mutiny on the Bounty* to *The Informer*. I used to put on these little shows.

I didn't realize how much Sennett, the Keystone Kops, and Our Gang influenced my thinking until I did my first film. I was out here in Los Angeles, doing the first Judy Garland special for TV. Tony Curtis came to one of the rehearsals, and he asked me if I wanted to do a film. It was a movie called *Forty Pounds of Trouble* at Universal, and it involved a chase scene. They were trying to get Walt Disney to allow them to shoot in Disneyland. It would be the first film—strangely, not a Disney film—that would

shoot in Disneyland. The way the scene was written in the script it was just a short chase, basically just a paragraph. I went to Tony, and I said, "Look, I'll do the film if you'll let me shoot for four or five days in Disneyland. I think the park is the second star of the film." I told him I wanted to do a Mack Sennett piece with the chase.

Well, we made the deal. As I remember, we paid $50,000 to Walt Disney, and that gave me the chance to do a Keystone Kops chase at Disneyland. I now realize that this desire came from when I was six or seven years old and watched all those Keystone Kops chases. Those childhood memories are embedded in your psyche. I had so much fun on that film, making those childhood memories come to reality.

When we think about the great moments, we all go back to our childhood and those formative years, because that's when we're most impressionable. This was all before television. We had nothing but movies and radio, and movies really were the main form of entertainment when I was a child. So it's all child-hood reactions that I was most affected by. ✪

The Keystone Kops

bringing up baby

fay**Kanin**

Fay Kanin, writer and producer for stage, screen, and televison, was a four-term president of the Academy of Motion Picture Arts and Sciences. She presently serves as vice president of the Academy and as chair of the Foreign Film Executive Committee. She co-chairs, with Martin Scorsese and John Ptak, The American Film Institute's Center for Film and Video Preservation and also chairs the National Film Preservation Board in Washington.

Kanin's films have drawn an Academy Award nomination (for *Teacher's Pet*, which she co-wrote with her husband, Michael Kanin) and Emmy, Peabody, Christopher, and Writers Guild Awards (for *Tell Me Where It Hurts, Hustling, Friendly Fire*, and *Heartsounds*, on which she also served as co-producer). Her Broadway musical, *Grind*, won a Tony nomination.

My first job right out of college was at RKO, where I spent my days writing synopses for executives who didn't have the time or desire to work through the material submitted to the studio. I made twenty-five dollars a week, but I would have paid *them* to be able to eat my brown-bag lunch on a bench in the small square in front of the Administration Building and watch Ginger Rogers and Fred Astaire and Cary Grant and Kate Hepburn and others of my heroes go by on their way to the commissary.

I met my husband, Michael, there, and when some years later we decided to build our first house, we discovered that both of us remembered and loved the wonderful early American farmhouse in one of our favorite old movies, *Bringing Up Baby*. We asked Van Nest Polglase, head of the art department, for stills and sketches, and our architect lovingly reproduced the house for us. And for a couple of dozen years, until we sold it and moved away, people used to visit us and say, "I have a feeling I've been here before," and we'd say, "You have—in *Bringing Up Baby*."

A few weeks ago, a friend who happens to live across the street from that house reported that it had recently changed hands again. "The new owners," she said, "are tearing it apart and rebuilding."

"Oh no!" I cried, "They can't do that. They can't destroy our beautiful house." I briefly considered extreme measures to prevent the desecration. I could throw myself in front of a bulldozer; I would get a petition signed by 50,000 leading architects; I would have it named a national monument. And then I realized why they can never really destroy it. Because I can revisit our house wherever in the world *Bringing Up Baby* is lighting up a big or small screen. I can warm myself at the great stone fireplace and, with Katharine Hepburn and Cary Grant, tread the oak-planked floors. Unless ("Oh no!" I cry) unless time, indifference, and neglect eventually destroy the movie.

There are certainly other more compelling reasons for preserving our great film heritage, but that happens to be mine. ✪

Charles Butterworth, Cary Grant, Katharine Hepburn, and May Robson in *Bringing Up Baby*, 1938

lawrence Kasdan

Lawrence Kasdan began writing original screenplays with the hope that it could one day lead to the chance to direct feature films. After graduating from the University of Michigan, he worked as an advertising copywriter in Detroit and Los Angeles, while trying to sell his scripts. In 1977, *The Bodyguard*, his sixth screenplay submitted to the Hollywood studios, became the first to be sold (it was finally produced in 1992). Soon afterward, *Continental Divide* was purchased by Steven Spielberg for Universal Pictures. Spielberg introduced Kasdan to George Lucas, who hired him to write what was to become *Raiders of the Lost Ark*, the second draft of *The Empire Strikes Back*, and the screenplay for *Return of the Jedi*, which Kasdan co-wrote with Lucas.

Kasdan's critically acclaimed directorial debut of his original screenplay *Body Heat* (1980) was followed by his direction of *The Big Chill*, a script he wrote with Barbara Benedek. In 1985, Kasdan produced and directed *Silverado*, based on a screenplay he wrote with his brother Mark. *The Accidental Tourist*, based on Anne Tyler's successful novel, was Kasdan's next project, which he produced and directed from a script he helped adapt. Next came *I Love You to Death* and *Grand Canyon*. He produced *Cross My Heart* (1987) and was the executive producer of *Immediate Family* (1989) and *Jumpin' at the Boneyard* (1992). 1994 saw the release of *Wyatt Earp*, directed by Kasdan from a script he co-wrote with Dan Gordon. Kasdan's *French Kiss* opened in 1995.

lawrence of arabia

Early in 1963, my brother and I rode a bus for ninety blocks down Miami Beach to see *Lawrence of Arabia* on the Lincoln Mall. We arrived seven minutes late for the matinee. My brother, who at nineteen was older and wiser than I, refused to go into the theater. Instead, we loitered in the streets for six hours so we could see the movie properly at the evening show, right from the start. As I endured the long wait, I thought my brother was crazy. But when the show was over, I knew I had done the right thing. As I stumbled from the theater, having seen the whole movie, I had a new hero. It was not T. E. Lawrence, but David Lean.

I emerged a most unusual creature, a fourteen-year-old boy who knew what he wanted to do with the rest of his life.

How powerful is a David Lean film? Well, it can start a person exploring that primary question: "Who are you?" One particular scene from *Lawrence of Arabia* did that for me.

T. E. Lawrence emerges from the Sinai on foot. His tragic crossing has cost the life of one of his two faithful boy servants. The surviving boy coaxes Lawrence up onto their single camel. Three tracking

shots bring them to desolate civilization, first in the form of barbed wire, then the bombed-out ruins of an outpost. The only sounds: the wind, the banging of battered doors, a whisper of score. The boy runs ahead through the rubble and returns, calling excitedly to Lawrence, but Lawrence sits on the camel, nearly catatonic, his face and robes so caked with dust that he appears finally to have become one with the desert, to have become a Bedouin. And the transformation seems to have sapped the last life from him.

The frightened boy throws water in Lawrence's face, washing away half his Arab countenance. His white English skin forms the other half of the mask.

"It's all right," he tells the boy.

They move through the ruins, and we cut ahead. As they approach the banging screen door, we hear the loudest sound . . . the horn of a ship? Here, in the desert? Lawrence and the boy come through the door and stop. After a beat, we see what they see: a steamship plowing through the sand dunes, a mirage-like clash of Lawrence's two worlds.

Lawrence and the boy appear over a rise. Only now does the score kick in, big. We cut to their point of view—the Suez Canal, steamship now in the distance.

Lawrence and the boy stare at the sight. Then a long shot of a lone motorcyclist riding along the opposite shore of the canal. Back to a wider two-shot; the boy starts yelling to the cyclist. Then, over the backs of Lawrence and the boy, the cyclist across the water stops his bike. We cut to a medium shot of the cyclist, a British soldier. He cups his hands to his mouth and shouts to them. The voice,

dubbed in later, is that of David Lean himself. What he shouts is this: "Who are you?"

Finally, only now, do we cut to a close shot of T. E. Lawrence's face. And once again, over his face, we hear the shouted question, which has been at the center of this epic film since its first frame.

"Who are you?"

It is the quintessential Lean moment. Its enormous force and resonance are achieved not only by the slow build of the sequence itself, but through all the sequences that have preceded it. With the audience the unsuspecting and lucky beneficiary, Lean has let the movie evolve inevitably toward this perfect, crystallizing image. ✪

Peter O'Toole in *Lawrence of Arabia*, 1962

a tree grows in brooklyn

gene**Kelly**

Famed as an actor, singer, dancer, and choreographer, Gene Kelly has also produced and directed motion pictures, television programs, and Broadway plays. Kelly began as a Broadway dancer, became dance director of *Best Foot Forward*, and staged nightclub shows for Billy Rose. After Kelly appeared in Broadway's *Pal Joey* in 1940, David O. Selznick signed him, but it was on loan to MGM in 1942 that he was cast in his first film role, *For Me and My Baby*, with Judy Garland. Kelly has performed in such memorable films as *Anchors Aweigh,* in which he introduced the film innovation of live dancers mingling with cartoons and received a Best Actor Oscar nomination, *Brigadoon, An American in Paris, Marjorie Morningstar, Inherit the Wind,* and *What a Way to Go.* He co-directed, as well as starred in, *On the Town, Singin' in the Rain,* and *It's Always Fair Weather,* and he directed *The Happy Road, Tunnel of Love, Gigot, Cheyenne Social Club,* the film version of the musical *Hello, Dolly!,* and *Invitation to the Dance.* Kelly also directed the 1958 Rogers and Hammerstein Broadway musical *Flower Drum Song.*

James Dunn and Peggy Ann Garner in *A Tree Grows in Brooklyn,* 1945

A scene from *A Tree Grows in Brooklyn*—in which Jimmy Dunn leaves Peggy Ann Garner, his daughter—is so sadly beautiful, I'll always remember it. Dunn plays a singing waiter, but he's a bum who spends all his money on booze. His wife suffers and scrimps, but despite all his failings, he has a heart. He and his daughter see beauty in a solitary tree that grows outside their window, amid the clutter of the Brooklyn tenement.

The scene that really touches me comes after they celebrate Christmas, when Dunn and his daughter talk about the lovely things in life. He tells her a story, and she falls asleep. He looks at her as she drifts off, and he realizes that he's ruining his little girl's life. He understands that, because of financial troubles, she won't be able to go to high school. At last, he makes up his mind that he'll go out and get a real job. That's the last we see of him. He leaves on this mission to get a job. It's almost medieval, as if he were going on a quest.

That scene is from the very last part of the picture. It's really for crying. It's beautiful, that scene of the father and daughter together for the last time. ✪

christine**Lahti**

This critically acclaimed actress has undertaken challenging parts on stage in *Three Hotels*, as Heidi Holland in Wendy Wasserstein's Pulitzer Prize–winning *The Heidi Chronicles*, in a revival of *Little Murders*, for which she received an Obie Award, the off-Broadway revival of John Guare's *Landscape of the Body*, David Mamet's *The Woods*, for which she received a Theatre World Award, and Tennessee Williams's *Cat on a Hot Tin Roof*, *Summer and Smoke*, and *Love Letters*.

On film, she has starred with Meg Tilly in *Leaving Normal* and in *The Doctor* opposite William Hurt. Other film credits include *Funny About Love*, *Gross Anatomy*, and *Running on Empty*, for which she received the 1988 Los Angeles Film Critics' Best Actress Award as well as a Golden Globe nomination for Best Actress. She has also starred in *Housekeeping*, *Just Between Friends*, *Whose Life Is It Anyway?*, and *. . . And Justice for All*. As Goldie Hawn's best friend in the World War II comedy *Swing Shift*, Lahti earned the Best Supporting Actress Award from the New York Film Critics' Circle as well as Academy Award and Golden Globe nominations.

Zvee Scooler and Richard Dreyfuss in *The Apprenticeship of Duddy Kravitz*, 1974

the apprenticeship of duddy kravitz and long day's journey into night

I never thought about movies when I was growing up. I never had any real experience with movies, except Saturday matinee horror films in Birmingham, Michigan, where I made out in the balcony with my boyfriend the whole time. I watched TV and really didn't go to movies, but *Long Day's Journey into Night*, Sidney Lumet's movie adaptation of the O'Neill play, which I saw when I was in college at Ann Arbor, transformed me. I remember riding home on my bike, sobbing. I became aware of the power that movies could have, and it made a tremendous impression on me. Yet I'd have to say that *The Apprenticeship of Duddy Kravitz* is, perhaps, my favorite movie. I recall this image of Richard Dreyfuss up at a beautiful Canadian lake, and he dreams of buying it for his grandfather, who, I believe, is a shoemaker. His grandfather had always told him that "A man without property is nobody," so he wants his grandfather to have some land before he dies. Of all the movies I've seen, *Duddy Kravitz* has had the most lasting effect on me. Seeing it was an epiphany. The movie was a lot less serious than *Long Day's Journey into Night*, and it touched a side of me that's a little lighter. I saw it in graduate school at Florida State. I was considering doing repertory theater at the time, but I wasn't wild about the theater program I was in. Seeing *Duddy Kravitz* was the catalyst that made me quit graduate school and move to New York. I loved the movie, and Richard Dreyfuss so inspired me. Here was this short and—I think he'll forgive me for saying this—kind of pudgy kid who wasn't typical leading-man material, and he was playing this incredible part. His performance was so honest. I thought, I'm not typical leading-lady material myself. I have never thought of myself as being particularly beautiful in that movie star kind of way, yet maybe there is something special about me in just who I am. Richard Dreyfuss had found what is special in him, and maybe I should just go and explore to try to find it in me. That was just the stimulation I needed. I immediately called up some friends in New York and said, "I'm coming tomorrow." I just quit school and went. ✪

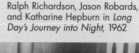

Ralph Richardson, Jason Robards, and Katharine Hepburn in *Long Day's Journey into Night*, 1962

angela**Lansbury**

Angela Lansbury's career spans more than half a century, during which she has starred in motion pictures, on Broadway (winning four Tony Awards), and in television's highest-rated drama series, *Murder, She Wrote*. Born in London on October 16, 1925, she was evacuated with her younger twin brothers to the United States in 1940 to escape the Blitz. Eventually, the family relocated to Los Angeles, where the seventeen-year-old Lansbury landed a seven-year contract at MGM after director George Cukor cast her as Nancy, the menacing maid in *Gaslight*.

Lansbury has appeared in forty-four motion pictures to date, including *National Velvet*, *The Harvey Girls*, Frank Capra's *State of the Union*, *The Long Hot Summer*, *The Manchurian Candidate* (for which she received a second Golden Globe Award, the National Board of Review Award, and her third Academy Award nomination), and *Death on the Nile* (a second National Board of Review Award). She made her Broadway debut in 1957 as Bert Lahr's wife in *Hotel Paradiso*, returned to Broadway in *A Taste of Honey*, then triumphed as *Mame*, earning the first of her unprecedented four Tony Awards as Best Actress in a Musical. She received the others as the Madwoman of Chaillot in *Dear World* (1968), as Mama Rose in the 1974 revival of *Gypsy*, and as Mrs. Lovett in *Sweeney Todd* (1979).

She was to find her largest audience on television, as Jessica Fletcher, of *Murder, She Wrote*. Lansbury was named a Commander of the British Empire by Queen Elizabeth II in June 1994.

a moment with clark gable

When I began to make movies at MGM in 1943, the studio lot was more open and accessible than film studios are today. As you walked around the MGM lot in those days, you actually had a sense of the entire process of filmmaking. When, for instance, you walked past the music stages, you could hear them recording background music. The dubbing room was in a very old building. I can still hear the clatter of people's feet as they went up and down those metal steps. As you passed that building, you'd hear the disembodied voices of the film stars, repeating the same lines over and over.

MGM used to promote itself as having more stars than in the heavens. You'd see these famous actors in the MGM coffee shop, which in those days was like the corner drug store. It was right across the street from where you got your boots polished. The great stars were always around, either in the drug store looking for magazines, or having their shoes cleaned.

But there was one star who for me shone brighter than all the others, one star totally apart from the rest of us mortals. That star was Clark Gable. To a young girl of eighteen, he seemed to have such charm and insouciance and sophistication, without any effort whatsoever. Gable also stood apart because he was the one film star you never saw. He was not on the lot. World War II was still raging, and he was away in England serving with the Army Air Corps. But one morning in early 1944, in the midst of filming *National Velvet*, I was all alone, walking down one of those wide MGM roadways, when coming toward me I saw—to my immense excitement—Clark Gable. He was just back from England, dressed in his Army Air Corps uniform, complete with cap, and looking like everybody's dream of a military man. He was walking with a small group of people, but I didn't notice any of the others. I only had eyes for The King. I caught my breath and kept on walking. But as I passed him, by golly if he didn't stop and say, "Angela Lansbury."

I was dumbstruck. I couldn't believe he even knew who I was. But I found my voice and answered, "Yes?"

Then, to my amazement, he asked, "May I speak with you for a moment? I want to ask if you could possibly help me out with something that I'm working on here at the studio?"

My mind was racing: Clark Gable wants me to help him . . . and I have no witnesses. No one is going to believe me when I tell them this happened.

He said, "You know, I'm making documentaries for the Air Corps, and I'm in the process of dubbing one, and I need some help. How about us ducking into the coffee shop?"

I thought to myself, my God, the coffee shop! People are going to see me sitting with Clark Gable in the coffee shop. I can't believe this.

As it happened, I was free at the moment, so he said good-bye to the people he was with and escorted me around the corner to the good old MGM coffee shop. We sat at the counter. I remember thinking to myself, the women who work behind the counter know all the stars. They know Clark Gable, and they're not thrown by him at all. So I must make a great effort to be very calm.

I ordered coffee, and he ordered coffee.

He said, "Would you like a doughnut?"

I said, "Wow, yes. I'd *love* a doughnut."

Then he said, "I don't want to keep you, but I'm just in the process of dubbing one of my documentaries, and I need an English girl to do some voice-overs of someone laughing in a field." He went on to explain, "This documentary is about young trainees at an airfield in England. They're having fun, and they're taking some of the local girls out, and they're all in this field, walking and playing ball, and the girls are laughing and carrying on. Do you think you could do some of the voices?"

So I said, "Well, thank you very much. Yes, I think I could do that."

We finished our doughnuts and our coffee, and he couldn't have been more of a gentleman. He was so respectful of me, which was terribly dear of him, because he knew that I was a very shy young English girl and fairly new on the lot.

And I did as he asked. We met in the dubbing room, and Clark Gable directed me as I performed the voice-overs.

So that was my experience with a great, great star. Subsequently, the great excitement for me was that we were going to make a movie at MGM to be called *Angels Flight*, in which I would have played opposite Gable. The film was never made, and I never got to act with him. But if I had, it would have been a dream come true. ✪

Clark Gable, in U.S.A.A.F. uniform,
with Army training film he shot,
1944

jack**Lemmon**

The first actor ever to win Oscars as both Best Actor (*Save the Tiger*) and Best Supporting Actor (*Mr. Roberts*), Jack Lemmon also earned Best Actor awards at Cannes for *The China Syndrome* and *Missing*, making him the first man ever to win twice at the famous international film festival.

Lemmon has given some five hundred television performances, almost all of them live, and made his 1953 Broadway debut in *Room Service*. He started his screen career in a pair of Judy Holliday pictures, *It Should Happen to You* and *Phfft*, then found himself nominated for the Best Actor Oscar three times in five years, for *Some Like It Hot*, *The Apartment*, and *Days of Wine and Roses*.

Lemmon especially loves to work with friends like Billy Wilder and Walter Matthau. In *Buddy, Buddy*, Lemmon worked under Wilder's direction for the seventh time, and acted with Matthau for the fourth. Wilder previously directed some of Lemmon's most memorable screen outings from 1958 to 1974: *Some Like It Hot*, *The Apartment*, *Irma La Douce*, *The Fortune Cookie*, *Avanti*, and *The Front Page*. *The Odd Couple*, co-starring Matthau, *Mass Appeal*, *That's Life*, *Dad*, Oliver Stone's *JFK*, David Mamet's *Glengarry Glen Ross*, which earned Lemmon the Venice Film Festival award for Best Actor and the Best Actor award from the National Board of Review, *Grumpy Old Men*, again with Matthau, and *A Life in the Theatre* rank among the actor's most impressive film performances.

Laurence Olivier and Robert Donat in *The Magic Box*, 1952

the magic box

One that has always hit me is from *The Magic Box*, an English film with Robert Donat, Laurence Olivier, Ralph Richardson—a whole lot of British actors in it.

It's about the invention of the movie camera. Robert Donat, who was always one of my two or three favorite actors ever, plays the inventor William Friese-Green. When he creates his invention, this lonely and obscure man doesn't have anybody to tell. He runs out to the street, sees a bobby, and grabs him, pulling at him and forcing him to come up to his room while he hand cranks the camera to show him how it works.

This scene epitomized something I always admired in acting, especially in the work of Robert Donat and Spencer Tracy: the ability to make it seem that the words they speak have never been spoken before, at least not by them. It was always Take One to me. Donat always had an immediacy, an urgency, and a level of energy that made me believe it was all just plain happening. It really began to hit me after I started acting and found out what you had to go through. That's the real trick on film: to make it seem that it is happening for the first time. That scene from *The Magic Box* keeps coming back to me, year after year, when Donat pulled in Olivier, the bobby, to see his invention. The excitement that he had and the immediacy of the moment, it still gives me chills. ✪

the mummy

barryLevinson

Born and raised in Baltimore, Academy Award–winning director, screenwriter, and producer Barry Levinson has used his hometown as the setting for three widely praised features: *Diner*, *Tin Men*, and *Avalon*. Levinson returned to Baltimore to film the *Homicide: Life on the Street* televison series, which earned him an Emmy for Best Individual Director of a Drama Series.

Levinson wrote for several television variety shows, including *The Carol Burnett Show*, for which he won two Emmys. A meeting with Mel Brooks led Levinson to collaborate on the features *Silent Movie* and *High Anxiety*.

Levinson was awarded the 1988 Best Director Oscar for the multi-award–winning *Rain Man*, and in 1991, *Bugsy*, directed and produced by Levinson, was nominated for ten Academy Awards. As a screenwriter, Levinson has received three Academy Award nominations, for *. . . And Justice for All*, *Diner*, and *Avalon*. Levinson's other directorial credits include *The Natural*; *Good Morning, Vietnam*; *Toys*; and *Disclosure*.

Boris Karloff in *The Mummy*, 1932

My most memorable scene is from what was not a particularly great movie. When we were kids, my cousin Eddie and I used to go up to the Gwyn Theater almost every Saturday. This was in the late forties. The theater was just up the street from us. It specialized in Republic and Monarch films—"B" stuff. We'd go at eleven o'clock with a lunch and wouldn't come out until 4:30. It didn't matter what was playing. They used to bring back old movies; we didn't know they were old, though.

One time we saw *The Mummy*, with Boris Karloff, an early thirties movie. That movie really stayed with me, though I haven't seen it since. *The Mummy* was all bandaged up. He dragged his leg. He had his hand stretched out like he was coming to strangle you to death. We were so taken with that film that, afterwards, we had this lengthy discussion about how the Mummy could actually catch anyone. If he had to drag his foot like that, how would he catch a kid who is much more mobile and fast?

Then, after we had settled down and felt safe, Eddie said to me, "The problem is, sometime or other we have to go to sleep, and the Mummy never sleeps."

"Oh, God, " I thought.

While *The Mummy* always stood in my mind, I can't even evaluate it, because I haven't seen it since. The interesting thing about childhood recollections is that you hold onto something that may have been in the movie only for a few seconds. What was actually shown and what I remember might not even be the same. But I don't think that makes any difference. It's the impression you walk away with. My kids today are the same way. They will mention one moment in a film that does it for them. ✪

modern times

john**Lithgow**

Although it was his 1982 Academy Award–nominated performance in *The World According to Garp* that first brought John Lithgow national attention, he made his acting debut on stage at age six in *Henry VI, Part 3*. A Harvard graduate, Lithgow won a Fulbright Scholarship and used it to study at the London Academy of Music and Dramatic Art. He went on to win both Tony and Drama Desk Awards for the Broadway production of *The Changing Room* and to star in the Tony-winning *M. Butterfly*. He was nominated for a Best Actor Tony, as well as a Drama Desk Award, for his performance in *Requiem for a Heavyweight*. He has also earned Emmy and Cable ACE Awards.

Lithgow received his second Oscar nomination for *Terms of Endearment* (1983). His other film credits include *All That Jazz*, *Footloose*, *Buckeroo Bonzai*, *Cliffhanger*, *Princess Caraboo*, *The Pelican Brief*, *Memphis Belle*, *At Play in the Fields of the Lord*, and *A Good Man in Africa*.

Charles Chaplin in *Modern Times*, 1936

When I was a child, there was a moment when I almost died laughing, and it happened when I was at the movies. It was during a scene in *Modern Times*, when Charlie Chaplin, spasmodically tightening rivets on a factory assembly line, was used as a guinea pig to try out a mechanical lunch machine. If Charlie could eat his lunch without taking a break, without even using his hands to feed himself, just think of the man-hours the company could save! As the assembly line chugged along, the lunch machine was wheeled up to him. It was a gigantic gizmo of a style best described as 1930s futuristic high-tech. At the level of Charlie's face was a lazy Susan with three or four devices to dispense food to him as he worked. There were cubes of sandwich meat, a cup of coffee, an ear of corn on a spindle, the obligatory slice of cream pie, and, best of all, a crescent-shaped sponge on a long arm which swept across to solemnly wipe his mouth after each course.

At first, the lunch machine performed flawlessly. Charlie worked while he ate, the assembly line hummed, the bosses beamed, and the machine's inventor preened. Emboldened by their success, the bosses sped up the assembly line. Then they sped up the machine. With the immutable logic of silent-screen farce, the lunch machine proceeded to go gloriously haywire. While the panicky inventor desperately tinkered, meat was jammed into Charlie's overstuffed mouth, coffee drenched him, pie was hurled in his face, and the ear of corn spun against his teeth like a lathe. The chaos built relentlessly, broken only by two or three grave pauses when the sponge slowly reached over to dab Charlie's messy, mortified face. It almost killed me.

Looking back on that scene, and on scores of others almost as fatal, I've grown to understand and revere the fantastically disciplined craft that went into their creation. Chaplin, Keaton, Lloyd, and, later, the Marx Brothers and W. C. Fields were all master

vaudevillians. Long before they ever stood in front of a camera, they had performed in front of hundreds of audiences, millions of living, breathing, laughing people. It was their good luck that film came along before vaudeville died out. They could take their comic genius out of the laboratory of live theater and sell it in the vast marketplace of the movies. Although their brilliance humbles me, I can at least claim to have followed their path from the stage to the sound stage. For when Charlie Chaplin was killing me in a darkened movie house many years ago, he was inspiring me too. I wanted to do what he did. I wanted to act, not just for a camera but for a crowd. ✪

Charles Chaplin in *Modern Times,* 1936

george**Lucas**

the seven samurai

Creator of the phenomenally successful *Star Wars* saga and *Indiana Jones* series, George Lucas directed his first feature film, *THX 1138*, in 1970. In 1971, he formed Lucasfilm Ltd. In 1973 the filmmaker wrote and directed *American Graffiti*, which won the Golden Globe, the New York Film Critics, and National Society of Film Critics Awards, and garnered five Oscar nominations. *Star Wars* won seven Academy Awards, and Lucas went on to script *The Empire Strikes Back* and *Return of the Jedi*, which he also executive produced. In 1980, he executive produced Steven Spielberg's *Raiders of the Lost Ark*, recipient of five Academy Awards. Lucas was co-executive producer and story creator of *Indiana Jones and the Temple of Doom*, and in 1988 he executive produced *Willow* and *Tucker: The Man and His Dream*, each of which garnered three Oscar nominations.

The following year, Lucas served as executive producer for *Indiana Jones and the Last Crusade*, nominated for two Academy Awards and winning for Best Sound Design. The Lucas-produced television series *The Young Indiana Jones Chronicles*, won the 1993 Banff Award for Best Continuing Series, a 1993 Golden Globe nomination for Best Dramatic Series, an Angel Award for Quality Programming, and ten Emmy awards.

The most memorable moment for me is the final battle scene in *The Seven Samurai*, where Toshiro Mifune leads the farmers in battle against the bandits. Obviously, it's a cumulative effect, with the entire story leading up to it, especially the preceding scene. How that scene played off the end battle scene, when Mifune led the farmers against the bandits, is what I'd consider my most illuminating movie moment.

The scene preceding the battle is set inside a mill. There's a fire going. Toshiro Mifune plays this kid who gets involved with the experienced Samurai. He's pretending to the farmers that he's a Samurai, but he's actually from humble farmer stock. In this scene, he breaks down and admits that he is not a real Samurai. He gets angry with the farmers for being individualistic, for not working together, for hoarding food and things. He rails against the pettiness of the farmers. He's ashamed of them, and of his own background, for the small way in which they think. He tells them they have to rise above it, to take on the kinds of values, selflessness, and humility that he learned from the Samurai.

It's a scene where he goes back into his own past and, I think, it is the real turning point for him. He started out as a boisterous, self-centered guy who wanted to be a Samurai for all the wrong reasons, because he wanted to be important. But the Samurai lessons have taken hold with him. He has learned humility from them, and it's at this point that he

actually becomes a Samurai himself—if not in fact, then in spirit.

This moment connects to the very exciting moment that follows, in which the bandits attack the village, and Mifune and the farmers fight to defend it. It's a very powerful battle scene in the rain. The fervor with which Mifune fights, even in his slightly clumsy way, has a real poignancy to it.

The way Kurosawa shoots the battle itself is very moving. He uses a lot of long lenses. It's very intense, partially because there's so much emotion behind all of the characters. Most of the movie is spent developing the character of each of the seven Samurai. Each one is protecting the villagers for an entirely different reason. Too many times, action pieces are very impersonal. This, however, is a very, very personal action scene centering on the main characters. You're interested in these characters. You care for them. It's not just a lot of random action. It's filled with pathos, a story of real people struggling to survive. It's the pathos, the elemental struggle, that makes it so powerful. ✪

battle of the century

leonard**Maltin**

Even before Leonard Maltin became a familiar face as the film critic and resident movie buff on TV's *Entertainment Tonight*, he had established himself as one of the country's leading film writers and historians, author or co-writer of a dozen books and editor of or contributor to some twenty more. His annual *Leonard Maltin's Movie and Video Guide* has celebrated more than twenty-five years in print.

Maltin is also host of the daily syndicated radio program, *Leonard Maltin on Video*, and has written a number of television specials, including *Fantasia: The Creation of a Disney Classic*, as well as hosted, produced, and scripted several video documentaries and compilations.

The first moment I remember in my movie-going "career" was the last scene of Walt Disney's *Snow White and the Seven Dwarfs*. (This was in the 1950s, during one of its periodic reissues.) My mother took me to see it, and, in those days of continuous showings, she pulled me into the theater as the film was ending, so we could be seated for the next performance. That's how I saw the last scene first!

Just a few years later, my parents took me to another film that definitely changed my life. It was Robert Youngson's 1958 compilation feature *The Golden Age of Comedy*. I had seen silent films before, as various comedy shorts were run on TV in those days, but watching the best of them collected together—on a big movie screen, not a seventeen-inch box, and with an audience around me sharing the laughter—was a revelation. The sequence that put me away was the gigantic pie fight in Laurel and Hardy's 1927 comedy *Battle of the Century*. Many others have staged pie-throwing melees since then, notably Blake Edwards in his heavy-handed homage to Laurel and Hardy, *The Great Race* (1965), but few have managed to draw the laughs that this one did (at least from me). That's because, as producer Hal Roach once put it, "It isn't pie-throwing that's funny. It's who

111

is throwing the pie, and who is being hit with the pie." When, in the midst of the comic chaos of *Battle of the Century* (in which scores of people and literally hundreds of pies are involved), a well-dressed dowager calmly surveys the scene, lowers her lorgnette, and is suddenly creamed in the face, it is very funny indeed.

This scene, and the rest of *The Golden Age of Comedy*, filled to the brim with ingenious and eye-popping gags from Hal Roach and Mack Sennett comedies, struck a chord in me. I went to the library and came home with Mack Sennett's *King of Comedy*, the first movie book I ever read. I moved on to John McCabe's loving biography, *Mr. Laurel and Mr. Hardy*. And I was hooked for life.

In later years, I became friendly with Robert Youngson and John McCabe, and I got to thank them for the seeds they had planted in me. As for the films themselves, I've never lost my love for silent comedy—or for *Battle of the Century*. ✪

the pride of the yankees

garry**Marshall**

Garry Marshall is the creator and producer of fourteen television series, including *The Odd Couple, Happy Days, Laverne & Shirley,* and *Mork and Mindy.* His TV shows, some of the longest-running and most celebrated sitcoms in American televison history, have won four Golden Globe Awards and seven Emmys. Marshall acts in a recurring role as head of a fictional television network on the *Murphy Brown* TV series and has appeared in several movies, including *The Escape Artist, Lost in America, Soapdish,* and *A League of Their Own.*

Marshall made his feature film directorial debut with *Young Doctors in Love* and has since directed *Exit to Eden, Beaches, Nothing in Common, The Flamingo Kid, Frankie and Johnny, Overboard,* and *Pretty Woman,* starring Julia Roberts and Richard Gere.

In 1990, Marshall received the Lifetime Creative Achievement Award from the American Comedy Awards. His autobiography, *Wake Me When It's Funny,* was published in 1995.

As a kid growing up in the forties and early fifties, I was under the impression that movies were either westerns you cheered at, Three Stooges and cartoons you laughed at, boring adult pictures you slept through, or Disney pictures your parents took you to so you could see a raccoon lick a duck.

The first movie I went to that made me feel like an adult was *The Pride of the Yankees.* I was a devout Yankees fan and rooted for and watched the war-years teams and the world championship Yankee teams of the late forties and fifties. However, I'd never seen a movie about baseball, and when my Grandpa Willie took me to see *The Pride of the Yankees,* I thought I'd see great baseball footage of guys hitting and catching balls.

Then, as I watched Gary Cooper go through Columbia University and marry Theresa Wright, I became hypnotized by the story. I never ever saw the Larrupin' Lou Gehrig play, but I totally loved him halfway through this film. The Yankees uniform, the real Babe Ruth (not William Bendix or John Goodman with a fake nose, but the *real* Babe Ruth), and Yankee Stadium itself were all in the picture. Finally, when Cooper, as Gehrig, came out and gave his retirement speech at home plate, and the microphone echoed in the vast stadium, I cried for the first time at a movie. I didn't cry at Bambi (a silly cartoon deer with a clumsy mother) or at Shirley Temple (bad hair, no boobs), but at a great baseball player, standing there dying and saying: "I'm the luckiest man . . ." That was something to cry over. I was embarrassed at first, but when I looked over and saw my Grandpa was crying, too, I knew it was okay.

Years later, many comedians in my field of comedy

Gary Cooper in *The Pride of the Yankees*, 1942

still made fun of that speech because of the "echo" effect, and it was funny to me later, too. Still, the farewell speech in *The Pride of the Yankees*, a poignant and heartfelt moment, allowed me to think that appropriate sentiment had a place in my future viewing experience and in my work. It also taught me to appreciate and understand irony. Here was this ballplayer they called the "Iron Horse," and he was leaving the game sick after playing the most games in a row of any player in history.

What truly amazed me as a kid was that I did not know these people in the movie, yet I was so moved. I'll always remember Gary Cooper as Lou Gehrig—old Yankee Number 4, giving his farewell speech at home plate—as the first time I was touched, not by flesh-and-blood humans, but by celluloid. ✪

rebel without a cause

marsha**Mason**

Marsha Mason began her acting career in New York City on and off Broadway and began her film career with Paul Mazursky's *Blume in Love* (1973). Her second feature, *Cinderella Liberty* (1974), earned an Academy Award nomination for Best Actress and a Golden Globe Award. Other feature performances include *Promises in the Dark*, *Murder by Death*, and *Max Dugan Returns*. Mason was nominated again for an Academy Award for her roles in *The Goodbye Girl* (which won a second Golden Globe), *Only When I Laugh*, and *Chapter Two*.

When she is not working, Mason races in SCCA-sanctioned competitions and the NASPORT series. The actress finished second in her division in 1993.

It's 1955, a warm, muggy day in St. Louis. I'm dressed in a pastel sleeveless dress with white gloves and white shoes and a white purse. We have just come from the "Big Sister Little Sister" luncheon, and several of us have decided to go to the movies. I am very excited because I feel so grown up, starting high school in the fall, and I am feeling fairly secure about what I am wearing and how my hair looks. I am worried that the perspiration under my arms will show and that my "Big Sister" might not like me. I don't really know her. She's already in high school and seems so different from me. I don't remember her name now or what she looked like, but I do remember sitting down in the darkened theater gratefully feeling the chilled air under my arms, and I remember the prickly plush seat scratching the back of my knees as *Rebel Without a Cause* began.

It is at this moment that my life takes an extraordinary turn. The title is meant for me. I feel like a rebel without a cause, but I couldn't put my adolescent feelings into words until that moment. My heart

James Dean and Natalie Wood in *Rebel Without a Cause*, 1955

feeling. And as I write this, my heart suddenly hurts, and tears spring from my eyes as I remember the sense of isolation and lack of understanding and compassion we experienced. I remember vividly the chicken race and the thrill I felt as I watched the speeding cars, and I so wished I could do that. Then came the extreme close-up of the jacket sleeve caught on the door handle. Then the close-up of the boy's face as he met his fate. I wanted to avert my eyes, but a voice inside said, "Watch. Don't look away."

Later that year or perhaps the following spring, I would act for the very first time ever. I got in the show because of a fluke. Sister Gabriel came to me because I happened not to have a scheduling conflict, so I was more or less drafted. But as I heard the audience gasp and sigh as I made my first entrance, I knew instantaneously that I wanted to do this for the rest of my life, and I also knew that I wanted to be as good and as truthful as James Dean in *Rebel Without a Cause*.

A couple of years later I would lose a friend, a handsome young man named Anthony. He was killed in a car accident. At his funeral I looked around the church at my friends and at Anthony's family, and I thought of *Rebel Without a Cause*, and I felt tied to something. A vague feeling, but it gave me momentary peace. Today, I race cars. ✪

thumps, and an ache constricts my throat, and I sit transfixed and hardly breathing. The tight friendship that Sal Mineo, Natalie Wood, and James Dean create for me makes me sad and happy. Sad that I don't share a friendship like that, and so gratefully happy now that I have met them and can vicariously share in *their* friendship. We are kindred spirits feeling all the same feelings. Up until now I didn't think anyone else would know. Their love for one another and their pain touches me deeply.

I am James Dean. I have met myself. Someone who is just like me.

As he cried, I cried. As his face and body contorted in his private agony, I knew exactly what he was

the informer

walter**Matthau**

Walter Matthau performed in many motion pictures before he did the Broadway play *The Odd Couple*, but it was this production that opened the doors to film stardom. Matthau went on to an Academy Award–winning performance in *The Fortune Cookie*, the first of several films he made with Jack Lemmon, who later directed Matthau to an Oscar nomination in *Kotch*.

Matthau has also starred in *The Odd Couple* film, *The Front Page*, and *Buddy, Buddy*, all co-starring Lemmon, as well as *Candy* with Marlon Brando, *Cactus Flower*, *Hello Dolly*, co-starring Barbra Streisand, *Plaza Suite*, *Charley Varrick*, for which he won the British Academy Award for Best Actor, *The Taking of Pelham One Two Three*, *The Sunshine Boys* with George Burns, *The Bad News Bears*, *I Ought to Be in Pictures*, Roman Polanski's *Pirates*, *The Couch Trip*, Roberto Benigni's *The Little Devil*, and *Grumpy Old Men*, among other films. He appears in a continuing series of made-for-TV movies, based on the television special *The Incident*.

I've seen John Ford's *The Informer* about thirty times. There are several scenes in it that stand out for me, particularly the last. It was a wonderful film. It captured character, and it captured mood. It was suspenseful, dramatic, and the language seemed to sing.

It's pure poetry. No dialogue for the first ten or fifteen minutes when Gypo (Victor McLaglen) is trying to get the thought out of his mind that there is a twenty-pound reward for Frankie McPhillip (Wallace Ford). He tears the wanted poster off the wall, and the wind blows the poster back against his leg. It's just spectacularly beautiful, everything that everybody says—the simplicity of it. You don't have to worry about who is doing what. Everything is crystal clear.

The scenes are magnificently woven together. Gypo and Terry are in the bawdy house, and Gypo remembers he has a meeting with the I.R.A. So he leaves, leaving Terry alone, and the madam asks Terry to pay for the drinks. He says something snotty to her, so she calls for Morgan the bouncer, who's a rough looking character. When Terry looks at this tough, he says, "Oh dear, oh dear, I have a queer feeling there'll be a strange face in heaven in the

morning"—the kind of poetry the Irish create, when they're sitting down or standing up.

There are so many poetic moments in the picture. Gypo goes to the wake of Frankie McPhillip, and he stands up, and the coins fall on the floor. You see the reaction of everybody to the coins falling on the floor. The way John Ford showed this was magnificent: a poetry of faces, and it must have taken five minutes.

Suddenly, someone comes over to Gypo and says "You don't seem to be in any need of money tonight, Gypo." Gypo grabs him and says, "What do you mean by that?" Beautiful moments.

The scene at the end of the picture is the one that gets me the most. It's the scene where Gypo is full of bullets, and he comes staggering into the church where Frankie McPhillip's mother (Una O'Connor) is praying. Gypo comes up to the old woman, and he says, "'Twas I who informed on your son, Mrs. McPhillip, but I didn't know what I was doing." She says, "Oh, I'm sure you didn't know what you were doing, Gypo. I forgive you, Gypo. " He looks up to the roof and says, "Frankie, your mother forgives me."

Marvelous. Even as I recall this now, I'm getting goose bumps. ✪

Victor McLaglen in *The Informer*, 1935

born yesterday

cathy**Moriarty**

Cathy Moriarty burst onto the film scene in 1980, starring—at age seventeen—opposite Robert De Niro in Martin Scorcese's Academy Award–winning drama, *Raging Bull*, and earning nominations for an Oscar, two Golden Globes, and a British Academy Award. This performance was followed by roles in such diverse films as the comedy *Neighbors*; the independent feature *White of the Eye*; *Kindergarten Cop*; *Soapdish*; *The Gun in Betty Lou's Handbag*; *Another Stakeout*; *Me and the Kid*; *The Mambo Kings*; *Matinee*; Steven Spielberg's *Casper*, based on the popular friendly ghost;

Pontiac Moon; *Forget Paris*, with Billy Crystal; and the indepedent feature, *Opposite Corners*.

My favorite movie moment was from a movie I saw when I was growing up, *Born Yesterday* with Judy Holliday. I thought there was nobody in the world like her. She could do drama, comedy, everything. It became my all-time favorite movie. I saw it on TV at my mom's house when I was fourteen. "Mom, I just have to be an actress," I told her.

She said, "That's nice, Cathy."

The scene that made the greatest impression on me was when Judy Holliday finally gets mad at Broderick Crawford and talks back to him. She tells him off. He was this very rich junkyard owner, and he acted like he owned her, too. He'd been constantly abusing her, belittling her, and, finally, she had just had enough and yelled back at him.

He was shocked when she stood up to him. It seemed to come out of nowhere, but it didn't. She had discovered her own confidence and had become more of a whole person. Now she had the strength to turn around and blast him. It was just perfect. I loved that. I guess I related to her part—I'm a little rough around the edges—and I just loved the way she told him off. She told him to shut up and called him a fascist.

Judy Holliday and Broderick Crawford in *Born Yesterday*, 1950

Someone finding their inner spirit and realizing their personal worth is what that scene is all about. People are not just what others make them out to be.

I've watched *Born Yesterday* many times. My fiancée just recently bought the tape for me, because he knows it's my all-time favorite. I was able to meet Garson Kanin once. It was on Valentine's Day in 1992. I got to have a drink with him and his wife and talk all about *Born Yesterday*. It was the best Valentine's gift I've ever had. ✪

the phantom of the opera

gordon Parks

One of the most noted photographers of our time, Gordon Parks began his career during World War II at the Farm Security Administration under Roy Stryker and went on to work as a freelance fashion photographer for *Vogue* and *Glamour*. In 1949 he joined *Life* magazine, where he worked as a photojournalist until 1968 and where he became famous for his stories about the leaders of the black revolution, articles later incorporated into his book *Born Black*. Parks is also the author of more than a dozen other books, including the classic *The Learning Tree* and *Voices in the Mirror*.

Parks began his film career in 1961, writing and directing the documentary *Flavio*, followed by the documentary *Diary of a Harlem Family*, for which he won an Emmy. He has also directed *The Learning Tree*, *Shaft*, *Shaft's Big Score*, *Super Cops*, and *Leadbelly*.

In 1988 he received the National Medal for the Arts, and in 1989 his ballet *Martin* premiered at the Kennedy Center in Washington, D.C.

For me, the most memorable moment in movies I saw as a kid. I grew up in Fort Scott, a little town in Kansas. I was about ten or twelve, and I went to see Lon Chaney in *The Phantom of the Opera*. I was sitting in what they called the Buzzards' Roost, the area that they assigned to black people.

I'll never forget the moment when Chaney unmasked himself, and you saw that skeletal face. I jumped, ran down the stairs, and out into the street, all the way to our farm.

As I started running down one street, I remembered that Mr. Allison had been shot there the week before, so I started up another street. But then I realized a gas main had blown up there and killed another man. So I chose the alleyway, which was adjoining our cornfield. Just before I got to the cornfield, my young mind saw Lon Chaney coming down toward me. He was about thirty-five feet tall. So I cut a swath through my father's cornfield to reach our back door. I burst through that cornfield, chased by Lon Chaney. ✪

Lon Chaney in *The Phantom of the Opera*, 1925

rashomon

daniel Petrie

Director Daniel Petrie has filmed the motion pictures *A Raisin in the Sun*, starring Sidney Poitier and Ruby Dee; *The Betsy* with Laurence Olivier and Robert Duvall; *Resurrection*, starring Ellen Burstyn and Sam Shepard; *Fort Apache, the Bronx* with Paul Newman; *The Bay Boy*, winner of six Canadian Genie Awards, including Best Picture and Screenplay (which Petrie wrote), and *Cocoon: The Return*, among others.

He has won Emmy and Directors Guild Awards for *The Dollmaker* and *Eleanor and Franklin*. Petrie also earned Emmy and Peabody Awards for *Sybil*, starring Sally Field. He has directed a number of other award-winning television specials, off-Broadway plays, the Helen Hayes tour of *The Cherry Orchard*, and *The Shadow of My Enemy* on Broadway.

Machiko Kyo and Toshiro Mifune in *Rashomon*, 1951

My only disciplinary problem as a child I attribute to the movies: I would often play hooky on Wednesday afternoons in order to attend the matinee. My parents were not amused. They subscribed to the generally held belief of that time, that classrooms and not cinemas were likely to develop young minds. The punishment: no dime allowance on Saturday, and therefore, no Saturday matinees. I got around that by getting up early Saturday morning and chopping wood for kindling, which I stuffed into burlap bags and sold for a nickel each to my "regulars," old folks living alone. I'd make enough for the tickets, and a box of Crackerjack besides. This was in Glace Bay, Nova Scotia, a mining town of 20,000, where there were two theaters, the Russell and the Savoy. If a Ken Maynard western was at the Savoy, and a Tim McCoy or a Hoot Gibson was at the Russell, I was in agony. When "The End" showed on the screen at one theater, I'd run as fast as I could to the other to sneak in for a glimpse at some admired star. More often, I'd be greeted by an exiting audience, which would include some of my buddies who'd take great

Toshiro Mifune *(left)* in *Rashomon,*
1951

Clementine, George Stevens's *Shane*, Orson Welles's *The Magnificent Ambersons.* All sublime. Then came the great foreign directors. "The director I'd most like to be is Truffaut, but the one who makes me want to quit is Bergman." I said that to a class of young filmmakers a dozen years ago, and it still applies. I love Truffaut's sweet sensibility, his ability to make the audience feel with the characters, all the pain and joy he wants us to feel. To me Bergman's *Shame* is one of the greatest war films ever made. It is beautifully acted, photographed, and written, and it resolutely avoids glamorizing what it condemns. But all his films have been masterpieces in greater or lesser degree. Three films had a never-to-be forgotten impact on me: one, another great war film, David Lean's *Bridge Over the River Kwai,* Fellini's *8½,* and Stevens's *A Place in the Sun.*

That's a long way of introducing the film that has a special place forever in my heart; which transported me in time and space, like no other; which showed me more than any film up to then the staggering potential of the art of cinema. That film was Akira Kurosawa's *Rashomon.*

Bosley Crowther, writing in *The New York Times,* said, "It is indeed an artistic achievement of such distinct and exotic character that it is difficult to estimate it alongside conventional story films. . . . The flow of images is expressive beyond words." High praise, yes, but hardly adequate to describe the wonder, the exaltation I experienced at the feet of this master Japanese filmmaker back on a sunny afternoon in 1951. Thank you, Mr. Kurosawa, for the towering contribution to the world of film and for the inspiration to young filmmakers everywhere. ✪

perverse delight in extolling the virtues of the movie I'd missed.

When my voice changed, so did my taste in pictures. Betty Grable, Alice Faye, Ginger Rogers, Deanna Durbin, Judy Garland were all my imaginary girlfriends. A little later came the heroes, Cooper, Gable, Bogart, Cagney, Stewart, Wayne, and Fonda. Their movies were a must. It was all escapism, pure pleasure. My parents fretted over such a waste of time, of money, such a waste of a mind.

Where exactly the change came, where movies became films, where thought became part of the process, I'm not sure. Certain films, certain filmmakers changed the way light was thrown onto a screen—no less pleasurable, but so much more profound. I became aware of John Ford's *My Darling*

robert**Redford**

the treasure of the sierra madre

Actor and director Robert Redford is a stage and screen favorite. He has starred on Broadway in *Sunday in New York* and *Barefoot in the Park*, recreating his stage role in the 1967 movie version of the play, having already appeared in the films *Situation Hopeless, But Not Serious* (1965), *Inside Daisy Clover* (1965), *This Property Is Condemned* (1966), and *The Chase* (1966). Next came *Butch Cassidy and the Sundance Kid* (1969), *Downhill Racer* (1969), produced by Redford's own Wildwood Enterprises, *The Candidate* (1972), the award-winning *The Sting* (1973), *The Way We Were* (1973), *The Great Gatsby* (1974), and *All the President's Men* (1976), among others. After a three-year screen absence, Redford returned to star in the romantic comedy *The Electric Horseman* (1979) and *Brubaker* (1980).

In 1980 he directed his first film, *Ordinary People*, winner of four Academy Awards, including Best Director and Best Picture. Redford next starred in *The Natural*, the Oscar-winning *Out of Africa* (1985), and *Legal Eagles* (1986). He returned to directing with *The Milagro Beanfield War* (1988), then starred in *Havana* (1990), *Sneakers* (1992), and *Indecent Proposal* (1993), and he directed *A River Runs Through It* (1992) and *Quiz Show* (1994).

He is the founder of the prestigious Sundance Institute and the Sundance Film Festival.

The Treasure of the Sierra Madre had a tremendous impact on me when I first saw it as a kid. There's a moment near the end of the film when the two surviving prospectors (Walter Huston and Tim Holt) both laugh. They have just lost all the gold they had mined, over $100,000. It literally blew away in the wind, and the Walter Huston character just starts to laugh. There is nothing else he could do. It was laughing in the face of all they had gone through—the bandits, Fred C. Dobbs's treachery, all the hardships. He just throws back his head and laughs, and this gets the other guy laughing, too. They sit down against an old wall and just roar. That scene had a great effect on me, laughing in the face of adversity, but it was the look and feel of the entire film that got me. I really believed they were down there in Tampico. I felt like I was in that place.

I remember sitting there in the movie theater thinking, "Oh, I see. This is what film can really be"—as

126

opposed to Disney and MGM and those kind of fluffy, colored spectacles—all those glossy films, with their kind of hyperventilated performing, which I did enjoy immensely as a kid. I went to Danny Kaye movies all the time. I thought they were the greatest thing in the world, and I'd do anything to get to a "Bugs Bunny." But *Sierra Madre* really hit me. This was different. This was far more interesting. I was just a kid and had no ambition to go into movies at the time—I was about ten years old—but it made a great impact on me. I still remember the feeling I had watching the ending of that film, how it awakened me to the potential of film. ✪

the graduate

christopher**Reeve**

Christopher Reeve rose to stardom as the high-flying man of steel in a series of *Superman* films. He has also starred in the motion pictures *Somewhere in Time, Death Trap, Monsignor, The Bostonians, Switching Channels, Noises Off, Remains of the Day, Above Suspicion, Speechless,* and *Village of the Damned,* among others.

Reeve has appeared in numerous TV movies-of-the-week, miniseries, and specials, as well as several Broadway plays, including *The Marriage of Figaro* and *The Aspern Papers.*

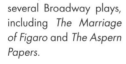

I'm particularly interested in moments where directing and camera technique support the story in some particularly apt way. The swimming pool scene in *The Graduate* with Dustin Hoffman is such a moment.

It was the celebration party for Dustin Hoffman's graduation, where his parents gave him scuba gear as a gift. Anne Bancroft says, "Go put it on, Benjamin." He very reluctantly puts it on and gets in the pool. Pictorially, that scene represents how his character is feeling in his life. It's symbolized by the shots when he's underwater in the pool: The distortion of the lens, and the fact that he can't hear any of the inane conversations going on above. He's just down there with the sound of his breathing through the regulator. It metaphorically suggests that he's kind of a fish-out-of-water, although here it's reversed: He's in the water, and all the land creatures are aliens. The image was so apt, so completely integrated. What is expressed

127

in that moment is Dustin Hoffman's isolation from his environment.

I was thirteen when *The Graduate* came out. I remember going to see it in Princeton, New Jersey, where I'm from. I saw it on a Friday evening with the college crowd, the Princeton students. I remember it being a very important experience for them because they identified completely with Dustin Hoffman. There was a tremendous rapport from the audience, a unification. They identified with this college graduate up there on the screen. It could have been any one of them up there. ✪

Dustin Hoffman in *The Graduate*, 1967

carl**Reiner**

romance

Depending on who you talk to, Carl Reiner is best known as a co-star on the legendary television program *Your Show of Shows*, or as the author of *Enter Laughing*, his first novel, or as the creator and co-star of *The Dick Van Dyke Show*, or as a director of feature films, including *The Jerk*, *All of Me*, and *Oh, God!* Or as father of actor-writer-director-producer Rob Reiner and husband of jazz vocalist Estelle Reiner.

Reiner began his career at age sixteen, enrolling in drama school for eight months and landing a part as a second tenor in an updated version of *The Merry Widow*. He won the lead in the national company of *Call Me Mister* and, after three more years in various Broadway musicals, joined Sid Caesar and Imogene Coca on *Your Show of Shows*.

His 1958 autobiographical novel, *Enter Laughing*, became the basis for a Broadway play and feature film, then in 1961, Reiner conceived *The Dick Van Dyke Show*, one of the best-loved sitcoms in television history. That same year, he wrote his first feature film, *The Thrill of It All*, for Doris Day and James Garner.

Reiner's other feature film credits as a director include *The Comic*; *Where's Poppa?*; *Oh, God!* starring George Burns; four films with Steve Martin, *The Jerk*, *Dead Men Don't Wear Plaid*, *The Man with Two Brains*, and *All of Me*; *Summer Rental* with John Candy; *The One and Only*; *Summer School*; *Bert Rigby, You're a Fool*; and *Sibling Rivalry* with Kirstie Alley.

*a*fter my first two film-going experiences, it is amazing to me that I would ever set foot into a movie theater again.

When I was maybe four or five, my parents, with no MPAA to guide them, took my brother Charley and me to see a picture about the legend of Doctor Faust. I don't remember the name of the movie or much else about it, save for the gargoylish face of the devil, lit from beneath his chin and laughing malevolently at me. I caught a glimpse of that horrible face before digging my head into my mother's lap and screaming out, "I wanna go home!"

My brother exhorting me not to "be such a baby" or my mother gently stroking my head and assuring me that it was "only a movie" did little to calm me. What finally did were the contents of an oblong, metal candy dispenser that was attached to the back of the seat in front of me. By depositing a nickel (or maybe a dime) into a slot and twisting a wheel on the side of the box, a tube-shaped container of non-pareil chocolates came sliding out. Because my parents were thoroughly enjoying the picture and neither wanted to baby-sit me in the lobby, they allowed me to have a full box of these chocolates,

which I finished while lying in my mother's lap.

It wasn't until we left the theater that I learned from my brother that because I was such a baby, I "missed the best movie of all time."

My second movie-going experience happened a few months later. My parents promised me that this time there would be nothing on the screen that would frighten me. And there wasn't. The movie was called *Romance*, and it starred Greta Garbo, one of the great actresses of that or any day. The music for the silent film was supplied by a pianist, who sat in a shallow pit at the side of the screen. Only the top of his head was visible, and I spent more time looking at him than I did at the screen.

After sitting through the first fifteen minutes of *Romance*, I saw nothing that kept my interest, and I longed for some kind of movement or excitement, and might have even welcomed the scary face of the devil leering down at me.

There was one stretch of film that I remember to this day. It was a medium-long profile shot of Greta Garbo standing behind a high-back arm chair, her chin tilted forward and her face looking terribly sad.

I asked my father what it was that was making her so unhappy. He said that if he told me, I wouldn't understand, so he didn't tell me. My mother seemed to understand the story, as every so often she would dab at her eyes with her hanky. Intermittently, interrupting Garbo's silent suffering, were cards with writing on them that were flashed onto the screen. I was able to pick out a few words, but not enough of them to help me follow the story.

I'm not sure of the name of the theater where I was forced to see this deadly slow-moving feature, but it was called either the Ritz or the Lyric, and was located somewhere on Tremont Avenue, south of Southern Boulevard in the Bronx. What I do remember vividly was a row of window boxes full of fake geraniums that rimmed the auditorium. To enhance the audience's enjoyment of this romantic movie, the enterprising manager had sprayed the window boxes with some kind of floral scent. It was supposed to smell like roses, the flowers that Garbo sniffed sadly, and often, during this endless film.

My father, who had a very sensitive sense of smell, had a difficult time with the heavy scent of something that was closer to doggy doo than to roses. When we first entered the theater, he said, "Feh! What is that stink?" He said "feh" twice more while watching the film and one last time as we walked up the aisle to go home.

We went to the Lyric/Ritz only that one time, but it was memorable. Too memorable. The next time I saw a still photo of Garbo, I smelled that smell again. Lucky for both of us that when I was sixteen and saw her in *Camille*, the memory of the odor of sour roses had faded from my mind's nose.

I think my taste for films was strongly influenced by seeing *Romance* and *Faust*. To this day, I find myself preferring to go to movies that do not stink and that won't frighten or bore me. ✪

Greta Garbo in *Romance*, 1930

it's a wonderful life

rob**Reiner**

Rob Reiner became a household name for his Emmy Award–winning portrayal of Michael Stivic, the son-in-law of Archie Bunker, in the landmark hit TV series *All in the Family*. Subsequently, he enjoyed great success as a film director with *This Is Spinal Tap*, a spoof "rockumentary" about a mythical heavy-metal group; *The Sure Thing*, a love story reminiscent of classic thirties romantic comedies; *Stand By Me*, about four boys coming of age in the fifties; and *The Princess Bride*, adapted for the screen by Academy Award winner William Goldman from his original novel.

In 1987 Reiner, with partners Alan Horn, Glenn Padnick, Andrew Scheinman, and Martin Shafer, founded Castle Rock Entertainment and directed for it *When Harry Met Sally*, which garnered a Best Director nomination from the Directors Guild of America, as well as an Oscar nomination for Best Original Screenplay; *Misery*; *A Few Good Men*, nominated for the DGA Best Director Award as well as for the Academy Award for Best Motion Picture of 1992; and *North*, a fantasy about an eleven-year-old boy's worldwide search for parents who truly appreciate him.

Donna Reed and James Stewart in *It's a Wonderful Life*, 1946

One of the moments that has always stayed with me is a scene in *It's a Wonderful Life* in which Mary Stone, played by Donna Reed, is on the phone with Sam Wainwright, who is calling from New York. George Bailey (Jimmy Stewart) has just come to visit her, and he's feeling awkward, being at her house. He leaves and then comes back to get his hat. She puts him on the phone with Sam. So the two of them are on the phone together, listening to this guy in New York talking about how they should invest in plastics. While the two of them are listening, George is falling in love with her.

She's always been in love with him, since the beginning of the picture—"George Bailey, I'll love you until the day I die"—but he's been resisting, resisting, resisting because he's always wanted to leave Bedford Falls, and he never wanted to settle down with her in a small town like that. Now he's finally given over to his feelings for her. He can't help himself. He looks at her, grabs her, and then he starts yelling at her, "I don't want to settle down, I don't want to get married." As he says this, he realizes it's hopeless. He starts kissing her.

It was all done in one shot, and to me it's one of the most powerfully emotional scenes I've ever seen in a movie. From what I understand, Jimmy Stewart hadn't been in a movie for a long time. This was his first movie after having served in the war. He came back, and he was nervous about whether or not he could do this. Apparently, this was the first take. They did one take, and that was it.

The first time I saw it must have been around 1971 or 1972. I had just started doing *All in the Family*, and a friend of mine asked me, "Have you ever seen a movie called *It's a Wonderful Life*?"

I hadn't even heard of it. After all, it didn't do very well when it came out in 1946. He had a 16 mm version of it and had a party where he screened it. I was just so blown away emotionally by it.

I got a copy of the film, and every Christmas I used to run it for friends and family. This was before they started showing it on television during the holidays. Every time I see it, I cry, and I've seen it now about forty or fifty times. ✪

Stewart and others in *It's a Wonderful Life*, 1946

day for night

evamarie Saint

Motion picture, stage, and television actress Eva Marie Saint's list of leading men is a who's who of the Hollywood elite: Marlon Brando, Bob Hope, Burt Lancaster, Richard Burton, Montgomery Clift, Cary Grant, Paul Newman, Warren Beatty, Richard Burton, Yves Montand, Gregory Peck, George C. Scott, and Tom Hanks. Her films include *On the Waterfront, That Certain Feeling, A Hatful of Rain, Raintree County, North by Northwest, Exodus, All Fall Down, 36 Hours, The Sandpiper, The Russians Are Coming,* and *Nothing in Common.*

A student of Lee Strasberg, she has won the Drama Critics Award and an Outer-Circle Critics Award for *The Trip to Bountiful* and an Oscar for *On the Waterfront.*

My favorite movie moment is from François Truffaut's *Day for Night.* There's something that's just magical about a movie set—the intimacy, the family-like feeling. Truffaut conveyed the whole experience of being on the set. It all worked so beautifully and in a sensitive way. The odd thing is that I usually don't like movies about the making of movies.

There were many wonderful moments, but the one that's touched me the most is when the Jacqueline Bisset character is doing her last scene. Although it's her last scene, the movie isn't finished. They will be continuing without her. After her scene, she says good-bye, and I'll always remember that look on her face. That sadness. They make so much of you while you're on the set, but after you've done your last shot, that's it. It's on to the next thing.

I related to that moment because I usually have a good time when I'm filming, and I'm never happy when it's over. That last shot I always find sad. I remember the feeling I had after I did my last scene in *On the Waterfront*—the first movie I was ever in. The director, Elia Kazan, said, "Good night, Gadge." And I said, "Goodnight? That's it? Excuse me." He said that was my last shot, and then someone took

Jean-Pierre Léaud, Jacqueline Bisset, and François Truffaut in *Day for Night*, 1973

136

a picture. There I am in my ski cap. My eyes watered over. I just couldn't believe that was it.

I was not prepared for it; no one had told me. I was not interested in the schedule, and I didn't realize it would end like that. Now I learn to look: What days do I work, what days am I off? I find out when my last day is, so I can be prepared.

Truffaut really caught what it's like to be on a set. The relationships are all so meaningful, and everybody is on such a high because they are doing something that they like. The catalyst is the project, which really brings you together, but when the shooting is over, you don't carry on with the relationships. It's never the same. ✪

red beard

john**Sayles**

With the release of his first feature, *Return of the Secaucus Seven*, in 1980, John Sayles established himself as a leader of the American independent film movement. Born in 1950 in Schenectady, New York, Sayles attended Williams College in Massachusetts and began to write. His first published story, "I-80 Nebraska," won an O. Henry Award. He followed that with a novel, *Pride of the Bimbos* (1975), then *Union Dues* (1977), which received a National Book Award nomination.

Sayles next found a place with Roger Corman's New World Pictures, for which he wrote *Pirhana* (1978), *The Lady in Red* (1979), and *Battle Beyond the Stars* (1981). Subsequent screenplays include *Alligator* (1980) and *The Howling* (1981). With $60,000 he had earned from screenwriting, Sayles wrote, directed, and edited the critically acclaimed *Return of the Secaucus Seven*. It was followed by *Lianna* (1983), *Baby It's You* (1983), *The Brother from Another Planet* (1984), and *Matewan* (1986). Sayles's *Eight Men Out* was followed by *City of Hope*, which won the Grand Prix at the Tokyo Film Festival. *Passion Fish*, starring Alfre Woodard and Mary McDonnell was completed in 1992, and *The Secret of Roan Inish* was released in 1995.

A gruff but warm-hearted doctor rescues an adolescent in feudal Japan from the house of prostitution where she has been beaten and abused. She has been so traumatized by this treatment that she can only kneel on the floor, eyes downcast, and scrub it with a brush in the same two-handed metronomic motion, back and forth, back-and-forth, back-and-forth. Very slowly, as the doctor (Toshiro Mifune) applies his kindness and patience, coaxing the girl out of her near-autistic state, her eyes rise from the floor.

One day, she smiles. It seems the doctor has effected a cure. The girl becomes part of the doctor's hospital, functional, though still somewhat shaky emotionally. And then we have the moment—an awful moment at first—a tight close-up of the scrub-brush on the wooden floor, the girl's hands gripping it tightly, scrubbing in the old metronome, back-and-forth, back-and-forth. Our hearts are sinking. She's regressed: Maybe the emotional damage is too deep. Then she jerks the brush into a beautiful free-form slalom on the floor, snapping water

Toshiro Mifune in *Red Beard*, 1965

with a flourish, and the effect is better than a dozen Hollywood orchestras laying down their finest uplifting schmaltz.

That director Akira Kurosawa can get you to feel so much with a simple close-up of a floor being scrubbed is a tribute to the genius of the moment, but also to all the scenes leading up to the moment, which make this particular scene work.

Red Beard is a very sentimental movie, but Kurosawa always does his legwork, always earns his sentiment, and pays it off in small physical details rather than synthesized bombast. ✪

great expectations

joel Schumacher

Joel Schumacher, whose films include the movie adaptation of John Grisham's thriller *The Client* (starring Susan Sarandon and Tommy Lee Jones), *Falling Down* (starring Michael Douglas), *Dying Young* and *Flatliners* (both starring Julia Roberts), *Cousins*, *The Lost Boys*, and *St. Elmo's Fire*, was born and raised in New York City. He began his career as an art director for television commericals and soon became a costume designer for feature films. Schumacher began directing with the television film *The Virginia Hill Story*, followed by the award-winning *Amateur Night at the Dixie Bar and Grill*, both of which he also wrote. *The Incredible Shrinking Woman* (1981) marked his feature film directing debut. In 1988 Schumacher directed the successful Chicago run of David Mamet's play *Speed-the-Plow*. His latest directorial projects include *Batman Forever*, starring Val Kilmer, Jim Carrey, Tommy Lee Jones, Chris O'Donnell, and Nicole Kidman, and *A Time to Kill*, based on Grisham's first novel.

My favorite movie moment made me want to become a director. It's a scene from *Great Expectations*, where the convict Magwitch jumps out from behind the gravestone and grabs Pip. I was seven, and my father had just died when I saw it. There was something about that movie that made me want to tell stories. I built a marionette theater and marionettes, and I started making up my own stories right after that.

That was a turning point in my life, that moment as Pip was tripping through the graveyard and the convict leaps out from beyond a tombstone. I nearly leapt out of my seat. I was with some friends. I grew up behind a movie theater in a very poor neighborhood, and we used to pry open the back door and sneak into the movie theater.

They would screen cartoons, Westerns, and other suitable fare for children, and then they would show an adult feature. *Great Expectations* was the adult feature. I don't think I knew what I was watching, and I'd certainly never heard of David Lean, but I fell in love with the movies. Something happened to me there. ✪

Finlay Currie and Anthony Wager
in *Great Expectations*, 1946

duel in the sun

martin Scorsese

A graduate of New York University, Martin Scorsese worked as an editor until his first feature, *Who's That Knocking at My Door?*, caught the attention of Roger Corman, who asked him to direct *Boxcar Bertha*. Scorsese's next film, the 1973 *Mean Streets*, launched his career. He has since directed the Academy Award–winning *Alice Doesn't Live Here Anymore*, *Taxi Driver*, *Raging Bull*, *The Color of Money*, and *Goodfellas*. He has also filmed *New York, New York*, *The Last Waltz*, *The King of Comedy*, *After Hours*, *The Last Temptation of Christ*, the "Life Lessons" segment of *New York Stories*, *Cape Fear*, *The Age of Innocence*, and *Casino*, and produced *The Grifters*, Robert De Niro's *Mad Dog and Glory*, *Naked in New York*, and *Clockers*, directed by Spike Lee.

A champion of film preservation, Scorsese launched Martin Scorsese Presents, a company dedicated to the restoration and distribution of classic films, in 1992.

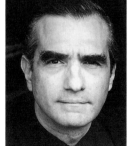

Gregory Peck and Jennifer Jones
in *Duel in the Sun*, 1946

It's not possible for me to limit my most meaningful movie experience to a single moment, let alone a single film. Where would I begin? *The Red Shoes*, *Citizen Kane*, *8½*, *The Searchers*, *Senso*, *The Leopard*, *The Third Man*, *On the Waterfront*, *East of Eden*, *Tales of Hoffman*, *Shane*, *Vertigo*, *The Wild Bunch*, *Bonnie and Clyde*, *Alexander Nevsky*, *Scarface*, *Viaggio in Italia*, *2001*, *Life and Death of Colonel Blimp*, *L'Aventurra*. I'm afraid the list would be quite long.

Instead, the experience of the movie theater itself is the first to come to mind. As a child, I remember being taken to the movies either by my father, mother, or brother. The first sensation was that of entering a magical world—the soft carpet, the smell of fresh popcorn, the darkness, the sense of safety, and, above all, sanctuary—much the same in my mind as entering a church. A place of dreams. A place that excited and stretched my imagination.

The first image I remember on a movie screen was in a trailer for a Roy Rogers movie. He was riding his horse, Trigger, jumping over a fallen tree. My father said to me, "That's Trigger. You know what Trigger is?" I said, "Yes, the trigger on a gun." And he said, "No, no—that's the name of the horse. I'll take you to see it next week."

Then, the first film I remember seeing by name: *Duel in the Sun*. The safety of the darkness of the theater was suddenly shattered by a bright blast of deliriously vibrant color followed by gunshots—the opening credits of

Duel in the Sun. It was 1946. I was five years old. It was a great sensual experience: the savage intensity of the music, the three-strip Technicolor, the sense of space (as only Vidor could create it), the use of matte shots, and ultimately the "duel in the sun" itself were all quite overwhelming. Frightened, I remember hiding my eyes during the finale, while the music burst over dissolves from Jennifer Jones on her horse to the bright yellow-white sun as the two lovers shot each other, and then as they died together in each other's arms. The hallucinatory quality of the imagery has never weakened for me over all these years. I guess the experience marked me forever.

Memories and experiences from the 1940s:

The camera moving in on a Technicolor globe as the godlike voice of Cecil B. DeMille introduces his epic *Samson and Delilah*. Slaves pulling giant stone statues, dynamically framed against a turbulent blood-red sky.

The excited expectation of walking in the lobby of a theater, glancing for a brief moment through the glass windows of the doors to the auditorium, and glimpsing cowboys sitting around a campfire at night, black-and-white night photography. I remember it was raining.

My mother takes me to see a B western, *El Paso*. John Wayne being taught by a Mexican how to fire pistols. In the montage, the light glinting off the long-barreled pistols, silver sparks that would find their way into *Taxi Driver* twenty-seven years later as De Niro plays with guns before his mirror. *El Paso* in outrageous CineColor—where the two prominent colors were turquoise and orange. Turquoise skies! Orange lamps! Surreal.

The Man from Colorado: psycho-noir western in Technicolor.

The thrill and wonder of seeing the Buena Vista/Disney logo fade up on a screen on a re-release of *Bambi*. The richness of the image. I could feel the brush strokes on the letters.

The brooding barroom fight in *Blood on the Moon* (co-billed with *One Touch of Venus*).

My father and I on a bus in Queens going to see *I Shot Jesse James* and me wondering, "Why is everyone just going on with their daily routines? Don't they realize *I Shot Jesse James* is playing?"

Robin Hood entering Prince John's banquet hall with a dead deer draped over his shoulders in a re-release of *The Adventures of Robin Hood*—in Technicolor.

The legs of the wicked witch sprouting from the bottom of Dorothy's wrecked home, then shriveling up and disappearing, in a re-release of *The Wizard of Oz*—in Technicolor.

Judy Garland throwing furniture and whatever she can get her hands on at Gene Kelly in *The Pirate*—in Technicolor.

The anticipation of wanting to see *She Wore a Yellow Ribbon*—then getting sick and missing it. The same happening with a re-release of *Stagecoach* playing two days only: Monday and Tuesday. All the adults I knew were working. I tried desperately to convince every one of my relatives to take me to see it. Missed that one, too. To this day, no matter how many times I see both films, I feel as if I've never really experienced them. I guess the time to see them had passed forever.

Then, in the early 1950s, the Third Avenue El takes me to 14th Street to see films like *Cry Danger* with Dick Powell—and *The Day the Earth Stood Still. The Red*

Shoes—age eight. The intensity of a real shared audience experience on a Sunday afternoon—several thousand people—all of us reacting to *The Thing*.

Leaving a theater in the afternoon—into the bright light of day—breaking the magic spell I had just been under—never being more aware of that spell being broken than when, at age ten, I left the neighborhood theater after seeing a re-release of *Gone with the Wind* in Technicolor.

Shane—at age ten. The death of the Martians in *War of the Worlds*—in Technicolor. The frightening power and intensity of *Pickup on South Street* in its first release. *The River*—Renoir at age ten.

The beauty of *Wagonmaster* in its first release.

The fun and thrill of witnessing real dual-projection 3-D on the first release of *House of Wax*. Then, in 1953, on a Saturday afternoon, seeing the curtain at the Roxy Theatre open and open and continue to open on a very wide new CinemaScope screen: *The Robe*. The wide image marking me forever as much as the three-strip Technicolor did, an obsession I was only able to indulge for the first time by making *Cape Fear*, in 1991, in anamorphic Panavision.

One of my great movie-going experiences—the night my cousin Michael and I crashed the New York premiere of *Giant* at the Roxy Theatre. Color, space, James Dean.

The overwhelming sense of authenticity—created through production design and music—in the spectacle of *Ancient Egypt: Land of the Pharaohs*. Hollywood in *The Bad and the Beautiful*. My brother and I at a neighborhood theater special Halloween double bill: *The Phantom of the Opera*, in Technicolor, and *The Invisible Ray*. Other double bills at the time: the re-release of *Four Feathers* and *Drums*, both in Technicolor.

Robert Donat in *The Magic Box*—in Technicolor—explaining "persistence of vision" through the use of tiny drawings in the margins of a book, which he flips, and the drawings come alive: moving pictures.

Mighty Joe Young and *The Leopard Man*—blood dripping under the door and scaring all of us kids. Montgomery Clift pounding on the door in Washington Square at the end of *The Heiress*. *Little Caesar* and *Public Enemy*. *Public Enemy*, the electric power of Cagney. A major influence: the use of contemporary source music—popular music of the day, not the usual film score.

For me, so much of the movie-going experience is linked with family. My father and I communicating silently by sharing these remarkable images and emotions together, leaving such an impression on me that, today, much of the desire and need to express myself on film comes from that. Over the years, some of that same communication and love has carried over to me and my children. Showing them these films—the same ones I saw—at just the time in their lives when I think they'd appreciate them most. (Most recently, *The Third Man* for my fifteen-year-old.)

I guess I'll always continue to try to relive the experiences I had back in my formative years, the forties and early fifties. I don't think I can be successful. The films haven't changed, but I have. Sometimes, as I watch them in 16 or 35 mm, a warm glow for a brief moment reminds me of those early times—the movies and my family—but then it's gone—quickly. I try to create it in my own films, but they can't compare in my heart to those early films I saw. Movement, music, color, emotion: movies. ✪

treasure island *and* a man called peter

ron Shelton

Writer-director Ron Shelton received an Oscar nomination for Best Original Screenplay for his 1988 directorial debut, *Bull Durham*, starring Kevin Costner, Susan Sarandon, and Tim Robbins. The sophisticated baseball comedy also earned Shelton screenplay awards from the Writers Guild of America, the New York Film Critics Circle, the Los Angeles Film Critics Association, and the National Society of Film Critics.

Shelton's first produced script was *Under Fire* (1983), followed by *Best of Times* (1985), starring Robin Williams and Kurt Russell. Shelton also wrote the screenplay for *Blue Chips* (1993), directed by William Friedkin.

Blaze (1989), Shelton's second directorial effort, from his own original screenplay, starred Paul Newman. He returned to the world of sports with his next features, *White Men Can't Jump* (1991) and *Cobb* (1994), starring Tommy Lee Jones —both of which Shelton also scripted.

Robert Newton and Bobby Driscoll in *Treasure Island*, 1950

Growing up a rock-ribbed Baptist, everything was forbidden: booze, cards, dancing, women, and movies. So all these took on a very attractive, exotic, glorious, and seductive role in my early childhood. Although a kid doesn't want to smoke or drink or chase women, he does like to go to the movies.

My most memorable movie moment comes from my earliest years, when movies were still a forbidden fruit. It's one overall memory impression from the first four movies I ever saw. To this day, I can't figure out why we were allowed to go to the four particular movies we were allowed to go to, but I can remember them.

The first movie I went to see was Ozzie and Harriet's *Two-Way Stretch*. We saw it in Los Angeles. We never went to a movie in my hometown, Santa Barbara. Maybe my father felt that if we were out of town, nobody would see us. So, we went to see *Two-Way Stretch*, a black-and-white movie. There was a girdle salesman in it, and the scene that always sticks in my memory is the one where they caught the bad guys by tying these girdles together between two trees. The bad guys' car couldn't get past; it kept bouncing off the girdles. Two-way stretch was the particular sales feature of this particular girdle. That was my first movie, and I'll always remember that girdle scene.

The second movie I was allowed to see was *Treasure Island* with Robert Newton. I think we were allowed to see it because it was a Disney movie. I loved it, and it inspired me to read Robert Louis Stevenson. I read all of his works.

The third movie I saw we drove outside of town to see. It was *Winchester '73*, a Western. We went to the drive-in in Ventura. Why we were allowed to see *Winchester '73*, I don't know.

The fourth movie-going experience I had was when we were in Taft, California, thirty miles from Bakersfield, visiting my grandmother. She was the most rock-ribbed Baptist of all. She took me and my little brother to a movie—and she didn't go to any movies. I was about eight, and he was about six. She took us to a movie by the title of *A Man Called Peter*, based on a best-selling book written by Katherine Marshall, who was the widow of a charismatic preacher named Peter Marshall. This book was not only huge in Fundamentalist circles, but it crossed over to the actual best-seller list, and a movie was made of it. So my grandmother thought this was okay. She took us to the Fox Theater in downtown Taft to see it, and we sat up in the balcony.

When *A Man Called Peter* finished, the second feature started: *Ma and Pa Kettle in Waikiki*. The titles came on, and my grandmother, thinking we should get our money's worth, started to watch, which she immediately regretted. The title sequence of *Ma and Pa Kettle in Waikiki* featured some hula dancers. She rushed us out of the theater, but she always felt that because we saw the hula dancers the damage had been done. Somewhere between the ending of *A Man Called Peter* and the "erotic" title sequence of *Ma and Pa Kettle in Waikiki* my film inspiration was born. ✪

Richard Todd in *A Man Called Peter*, 1955

lawrence of arabia

joel Silver

Raised in South Orange, New Jersey, Joel Silver attended New York University, where he produced his first film, a short entitled *Ten Pin Alley*. Shortly after graduation, he moved to Los Angeles, where he became an assistant to producer Lawrence Gordon. Within a short time, Silver was named president of the Motion Picture Division of Lawrence Gordon Productions. There he developed *The Driver*, *Hooper*, and *The End*. He served as associate producer on *The Warriors*, and he and Gordon produced *48 HRS.*, *Streets of Fire*, and *Brewster's Millions*.

The first Silver Pictures production was *Commando*, starring Arnold Schwarzenegger, followed by *Jumpin' Jack Flash*, *Predator*, and *The Hudsucker Proxy*. Silver has also produced *Lethal Weapon* (I and II), *Die Hard* (I and II), *The Last Boy Scout*, *Demoliton Man*, *Richie Rich*, *Fair Game*, a suspense-thriller starring William Baldwin and Cindy Crawford, and *Assassins*, an action-thriller starring Sylvester Stallone and Antonio Banderas.

I sat, ten years old, in a darkened theater, and was enraptured by the images of *Lawrence of Arabia*. To this day, I can recall the film with such clarity, as if it continuously plays on a screen in my head. If I had to choose one scene that affected me the most, it's the one where Lawrence is sitting alone after he has finished a meeting with his English superior and the Arab chieftain played by Alec Guiness. The Arab has been told his tribes cannot be armed because the nearest supply is in Aqaba, a seaside village occupied by the Turks. The British cannot approach Aqaba from the sea because the Turks have their cannon trained on the water. Crossing the fifty-mile stretch of desert by camel is also an impossibility. Although Lawrence's allegiance is to the British, his heart goes out to the Arabs. He sits under the shade of a lone palm and stares at the sun setting over the desert.

He makes a decision.

He whispers, "Aqaba . . ."

His determination grows stronger. He repeats the name with force.

"AQABA!"

Lawrence will lead the Arabs through the Nefud Desert to take the Turks by surprise. In this moment,

Peter O'Toole in *Lawrence of Arabia*, 1962

a shiver ran through my body. I watched the transformation of a man as he was about to become a legend.

Although I firmly believe that the spectacle of *Lawrence of Arabia* is one that will never be recaptured, I'd like to think that the spirit of O'Toole's Lawrence has in a way influenced the characters of my movies. I have attempted to infuse them with the same fortitude and willingness to face the impossible that David Lean forever ingrained in my head and heart with a single word—"Aqaba." ✪

steven Spielberg

One of the world's most respected and successful filmmakers, Steven Spielberg made his first movie at the age of twelve. Throughout his teens he directed several ambitious amateur films before enrolling in the film department at California State University, Long Beach. His

twenty-two minute *Amblin* (after which he named his production company in 1984) was shown at the 1969 Atlanta Film Festival and led to a unique seven-year contract with Universal Pictures, making him, at the age of twenty-one, the youngest director ever to land a long-term deal with a major Hollywood studio.

The Sugarland Express (1974) marked Spielberg's theatrical feature filmmaking debut, and was followed by *Jaws* (1975). *Close Encounters of the Third Kind* (1977) came next, and, in 1980, *Raiders of the Lost Ark* was the first in a trilogy of immensely popular action-adventure films directed by Spielberg and produced by George Lucas.

While Spielberg was directing *E.T.: The Extra-Terrestrial*, he co-wrote and co-produced *Poltergeist*. Other Spielberg projects include *The Color Purple* (1985) and *Empire of the Sun* (1987). His direction of *The Color Purple* earned him his first Directors Guild of America Award, and the film was nominated for eleven Academy Awards.

Spielberg followed these successes with the romantic fantasy *Always*, *Hook*, and the megablockbuster *Jurassic Park*. *Schindler's List*, based on the book by Thomas Keneally, presented the true story of Oskar Schindler, a Nazi war-profiteer who, at great risk, saved the lives of more than 1,100 Jews during World War II. The film won seven Academy Awards.

lawrence of arabia

P

Peter O'Toole as T. E. Lawrence in *Lawrence of Arabia* contemplates his future while gazing into a lit match. As he blows the match out, with the aid of eight frames of overlapping sound, he blows onto the screen a magnificent vista of the sun rising over the Arabian desert.

I saw *Lawrence* when it first came out in 1962. I was one of the first in line. ✪

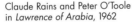

Claude Rains and Peter O'Toole
in *Lawrence of Arabia*, 1962

the good earth

rodSteiger

For memorable performances in historic motion pictures, critically acclaimed stage classics, and audience-pleasing television specials, Rod Steiger has received an Oscar, an Emmy, and numerous international film festival accolades and theater awards. After studying at the American Theater Wing, the Dramatic Workshop, and the Actors Studio in New York, Steiger appeared in some 250 live television productions, made his stage debut in the road company of *The Trial of Mary Dugan*, and his Broadway debut in a revival of Clifford Odets's *Night Music*. He made his motion-picture debut in *Teresa*.

Steiger earned his first Oscar nomination costarring with Marlon Brando in *On the Waterfront*. *The Pawnbroker*, *In the Heat of the Night* (for which he won the Best Actor Academy Award), *Doctor Zhivago*, *The Harder They Fall*, *The Loved One*, the film version of *Oklahoma!*, *Al Capone*, *No Way to Treat a Lady*, *Waterloo*, *W. C. Fields and Me*, *The Sergeant*, *The Chosen*, *The Life of Pope John XXIII*, *The Naked Face*, and *The Specialist* are among the more than seventy-two films in Steiger's distinguished career.

Paul Muni and Luise Rainer in *The Good Earth*, 1937

The most powerful movie moments for me are emotional. One I'll never forget is from *The Good Earth*, starring Paul Muni and Luise Rainer, who play a Chinese farming couple. It's one of those scenes with so much sheer emotion in it that it seemed to pick you up in the theater and fling you against the wall.

In this particular scene, Luise Rainer is pregnant, and the peasant farmers are looting the nobleman's palace. She's on the floor, reaching toward a small bag, when someone steps on her pregnant stomach. I jumped nearly three feet out of my seat in the theater when that happened. That scene was so scary—stepping on a baby—that it almost made me sick. It was the most shocking moment I've ever experienced in a movie theater. I can't forget it.

Later on, she looks in the bag and finds these two huge pearls. It changes her life and her husband's life. She loves him so much that she gives them to him, but he's ungrateful. He no longer pays any attention to her; he's got his concubines.

It's a wonderful film. I might have been in the Navy, around twenty years old, when I saw it. I'm not sure. I've seen it several times since, and it holds up very well. ✪

153

great expectations

donald**Sutherland**

Donald Sutherland, star of more than eighty feature films, began his career as a disc jockey at age fourteen. His first taste of theater came via roles in campus productions at the University of Toronto. Before earning his degree, he studied at the Royal Academy of Dramatic Art and made his London stage debut in *August for the People*. Sutherland spent the next several years performing on theater and television. His first feature film role, in *The Castle of the Living Dead*, was followed by a brief series of other horror pictures.

It was his fourteenth motion picture, Robert Altman's *M*A*S*H*, that first brought Sutherland international acclaim. He has also starred in *Ordinary People*, *Klute*, Fellini's *Casanova*, *The Dirty Dozen*, *The Eagle Has Landed*, *Max Dugan Returns*, Louis Malle's *Crackers*, *The Great Train Robbery*, *Backdraft*, *A Dry White Season*, *JFK*, *Six Degrees of Separation*, and *Disclosure*.

Anthony Wager in *Great Expectations*, 1946

They held the big meeting in the Capital Theatre. My father was there, trying like everybody else to figure out how to protect us from Nazi air raids. It was the early 1940s. My dad said the place was bedlam, that the yelling about what to do went on 'til some fellow he didn't know stood up and said, "Look, if enemy bombers fly over St. John, 90 percent of the time it'll be fogged in, and they'll have to go on to secondary targets. Right?" Bedlam. "The other 10 percent of the time they'll look down and see the city and think it's been bombed already. Right?" More bedlam. But it was so near to true they all agreed it was common sense to do nothing and adjourned.

155

My dad said when they walked out it was foggy and cold and damp. That was what it was always like outside the walls of the Capital Theatre, just off the King's Square, in St. John, New Brunswick.

Inside those walls, though: a castle. Truly. Stone walls, turrets, a moat, and what seemed like thousands of red, plush seats. I wasn't taken inside until 1946, when my mother decided I was old enough to go to the cinema, and that she would take me to see Charles Dickens's classic, *Great Expectations*.

She had a big hand. She walked me over the drawbridge, sat me on her right in one of those huge red seats. We waited. My poor brain couldn't sense whether I was in heaven or a dentist's reception room.

I don't remember the newsreel, or the trailers, or the cartoon. All I remember is the pages of a book turning and a voice telling me the story, and a boy running along a road, and posts like the ones in hangman's bluff but real, with chains, and the graveyard and the trees and the wind and the music and a tree again and putting flowers at the stone and him turning to leave, and then I screamed, and I was suddenly sitting in my mother's lap, watching Magwitch turn Pip upside down and my world with him.

I had suffered a sea change. I was another person in another life. My dreams had come true. I had found my touchstone, my proof-rock, my icon. On page 237 of Karel Reisz's *Technique of Film Editing*, Jack Harris, David Lean's editor, says the whole of that passage had been planned in cuts before shooting, eight shots running into Magwitch, "fourteen frames from the time the convict appears to the close-up of Pip screaming, Pip's scream starting four frames before the cut, at just the precise moment that the apparition is taken away from the audience's sight."

I don't know. I was airborne, a tribute to the Capital Theatre and the forgotten fighter-bombers. I was flying into the future and my mother's lap. My life was decided. I have been in love with Abel Magwitch ever since. ✪

Finlay Currie and George Hayes in *Great Expectations*, 1946

156

yankee doodle dandy

john**Travolta**

John Travolta received his first Oscar nomination at the age of twenty-three for *Saturday Night Fever*, a role that also garnered him a Golden Globe nomination and the National Board of Review Award for Best Actor. Seventeen years later, he once again won international critical and audience acclaim for his riveting performance in Quentin Tarantino's *Pulp Fiction*, earning a second Academy Award nomination, a Best Actor Award from the Los Angeles Film Critic's Association, and a Golden Globe nomination. Travolta received a Golden Globe Award for *Grease*.

His work for television includes the series *Welcome Back Kotter* and movies such as *The Boy in the Plastic Bubble* and Robert Altman's *Dumb Waiter*. His feature film credits include *Staying Alive*, *Urban Cowboy*, *Carrie*, *Look Who's Talking*, *White Man's Burden*, and the comedy *Get Shorty*, based on the Elmore Leonard novel.

Yankee Doodle Dandy made the biggest impact on me when I was a kid. I remember watching it on the living-room floor in New Jersey on *The Million Dollar Movie*, either channel 11 or 5, I don't remember which. It played on a regular schedule that week, every day at the same time. I went on a *Yankee Doodle* binge. I watched it over and over again.

Several scenes moved me. The scene in which James Cagney, who plays George M. Cohan, dances up the wall and comes down. The scene where Cohan brings his wife Mary (Joan Leslie) flowers because he's had to pass her over for a part in his own show. (She already knows it by the fact that he's giving her flowers, but she's not carrying on at all. She's just saying, "I know, George, and I think the other girl is just great for that part.")

Cagney's scene with his dad on his deathbed is very moving. He tells his father how much he loves him. Then the old man dies, and Cagney cries. It is hard not to have strong feelings about a scene like that.

When I got older, my favorite scene was from *A Man and a Woman*, where Jean-Louis (Jean-Louis Trintignant) drives back to meet Anne (Anouk Aimee) at the train station, and he knows that they should be

together. He drives through the Paris streets to beat the train to the next stop, getting to the station, and running down the stairs.

If I don't respond emotionally to a movie, then I usually don't have much of a memory of it. You take a ride on an emotional rollercoaster when you see a great movie. I remember being depressed in the early 1970s, and I didn't know how to get out of my funk. There were three movies that lifted me up: *That's Entertainment*, *Cabaret*, and *The Godfather*. They all meant something to me. I was a teenager, I was just trying to find my way as a human being, and those movies lifted me out of an emotional rut I was stuck in. But it was *Yankee Doodle Dandy* that came first for me. ✪

Walter Huston and James Cagney in *Yankee Doodle Dandy*, 1942

guess who's coming to dinner

kathleen Turner

Kathleen Turner made her steamy film debut in Lawrence Kasdan's film noir *Body Heat* and received a Golden Globe nomination for New Star of the Year and a British Academy Award nomination for Best Actress. For her role in *Romancing the Stone*, co-starring Michael Douglas and Danny DeVito, Turner earned a Best Actress Golden Globe. The threesome reunited for *The Jewel of the Nile* and *War of the Roses*. Turner also starred in Francis Ford Coppola's *Peggy Sue Got Married*, for which she received a Best Actress Academy Award nomination, Golden Globe nomination, and National Board of Review Award. Her starring role in John Huston's *Prizzi's Honor* earned her the Golden Globe for Best Actress.

She provided the sultry voice of Jessica Rabbit in Robert Zemeckis's *Who Framed Roger Rabbit?* and starred in Kasdan's *The Accidental Tourist*. Turner's stage work includes the 1989 Broadway revival of Tennessee Williams's *Cat on a Hot Tin Roof* and the 1995 Broadway play *Indiscretions*.

My favorite movie moment is from *Guess Who's Coming to Dinner*, when Katharine Hepburn shows this bigoted, high-society San Francisco woman out to her car after she meets Sidney Poitier, the fiancé of Hepburn's daughter. As the woman opens her mouth, Hepburn says, "Don't say a word," sweeping her hand upward in a V.

It's beautiful.

With this single motion, Hepburn sums up her attitude toward the woman. It shows her own spirit and shows that she isn't judging the woman, saying "you are an awful, despicable person." It is just a complete dismissal, executed in the confidence of doing the right thing, a supremely confident body gesture. It could not be misinterpreted: a dismissal, the perfect melding of gesture and thought. It could not have been physically expressed better.

The first time I saw *Guess Who's Coming to Dinner* was in a film theater in Venezuela. I was young,

160

between eight and thirteen years old. Of course, I didn't have any awareness of the acting technique Hepburn employed. But I was impressed by the melding of supreme confidence with humor. We laughed at the gesture. The audience understood it perfectly.

Hepburn was always very spare as a performer, but that was one of her best choices, a gesture I'll never forget. I just loved the clarity of that communication. Many years later, while watching the video of the movie at home, I could still savor the perfection of the moment. ✪

a man for all seasons

jackValenti

Texas-born and Harvard-educated, Jack Valenti has led several lives: a wartime bomber pilot, advertising agency founder, political consultant, White House assistant, and movie industry leader. Presently president and CEO of the Motion Picture Association of America, Valenti began his career with Humble Oil (now Exxon), then served as a pilot in World War II, earning the Distinguished Flying Cross, among other honors. He later co-founded the advertising and political consulting agency Weekley & Valenti, which was in charge of press relations during President Kennedy's fateful visit to Dallas. Valenti was in the motorcade on November 22, 1963, and, within hours of the assassination, became the first special assistant to the new president. In 1966, he resigned his White House post to become leader of the MPAA.

Valenti is the author of three non-fiction books and the political novel *Protect and Defend*.

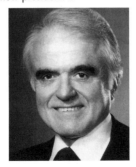

161

In Fred Zinneman's rare jewel of a movie *A Man for All Seasons*, written with insightful grace by Robert Bolt, there is a scene in Sir Thomas More's home in which his son-in-law, William Roper, berates More—played by Paul Scofield—for his reverence for the law.

"So you would give the devil the benefit of the law?" Roper cries.

"Yes," says More. "What would you do, cut a road through the law to get to the devil?"

To which Roper shouts triumphantly, "I'd cut down every law in England to do that."

More/Scofield's reply is one of those hinge covenants on which free, enduring nations turn.

"And when the last law was down"—More's voice is stern, commanding—"and when the devil turned round on you, where would you hide, Roper, the laws all being down? . . . This country's planted thick with laws, man's laws, not God's, and if you cut them all down, do you really think you could stand upright in the winds that would blow? Yes, I'd give the devil benefit of law, for my own safety's sake."

I've seen the movie at least fifteen times. I truly think I could understudy all the parts. Every American ought to watch this scene. We, too, often forget that when a tyrant first appears, he comes as your protector, climbing over the law's sometime awkward bulk to bring "order" and "discipline" to a frustrated society. For I know each time I hear Scofield's voice I am chastened by its passion, even as I am grateful for its truth. That is why Zinneman/Bolt's film is the movie industry at the highest point to which its creative spirit can soar. ✪

Paul Scofield in *A Man for All Seasons*, 1966

the kid

wayne Wang

Wayne Wang was born in Hong Kong and came to the United States to study painting. He changed his mind and studied filmmaking instead. His first film, the 1982 *Chan Is Missing*, was a critical success. Wang next completed *Dim Sum* in 1984 and, in 1987, made *Slamdance* with Tom Hulce, Mary Elizabeth Mastrantonio, and Harry Dean Stanton. He followed these features with the 1989 comedy *Eat a Bowl of Tea*.

In 1990 Wang returned to Hong Kong to make what he called "a down-and-dirty offbeat film," *Life Is Cheap . . . but Toilet Paper Is Expensive* and, in 1993, brought to life Amy Tan's moving and intricately poetic novel, *The Joy Luck Club*. *Smoke*, written by novelist Paul Auster and starring William Hurt, Harvey Keitel, and Harold Perrineau, was Wang's next project. The film led to his improvisational and experimental movie *Blue in the Face*, the concept for which originated during *Smoke* rehearsals. It stars Harvey Keitel, Roseanne, Michael J. Fox, Lily Tomlin, and Madonna.

i

It's hard to pick just a moment, but there's one that stands out from one of the first movies I ever saw as a child in Hong Kong. They used to show Charlie Chaplin movies all the time. They were some of my first movies. *The Kid* is one of the films that really moved me, made me cry, made me feel a lot of different things. All these things and without any dialogue.

The one moment I remember most clearly is the scene after the orphan kid has been taken from the Little Tramp and has been turned over to the authorities. The Little Tramp is very upset, and he sits down on a porch stoop where he and the Kid used to sit. He falls asleep and dreams. He dreams about heaven, with everyone, including him and the Kid, wearing angel wings. Everything is initially perfect, but then these bad people start showing up and messing with heaven. The fact that this idyllic possibility, heaven, was being destroyed in his dream by many

of the same things that occurred on earth told me something very important about life, about accepting a certain touch of reality in the world, and that things may never be perfect.

I was probably between four and five when I saw *The Kid*. I spoke very little English. That's part of the reason why those movies were so impressive; they cut across language barriers. I remember I loved going to see them. I used to ask for money for haircuts and then not get haircuts. I'd have a friend cut my hair and use the money to go to the movies. There were 5:30 shows in the afternoon that were really cheap. I probably saw *The Kid* with haircut money. ✪

Charles Chaplin and Jackie Coogan in *The Kid*, 1921

splendor in the grass

lesleyann**Warren**

Lesley Ann Warren began her career on Broadway as the ingenue lead in *110 in the Shade*, and first found stardom on the small screen as *Cinderella* in the television version of the Rodgers and Hammerstein classic. Warren studied with Lee Strasberg while appearing on stage in *Drat! The Cat!*, the Actor's Studio production of *Threepenny Opera*, and as Scarlett O'Hara in an English musical version of *Gone With the Wind*. Her first feature film was *The Happiest Millionaire* for Disney.

Warren's performance in Blake Edwards's *Victor/Victoria* earned her an Academy Award nomination as Best Supporting actress. She also won the New York Film Critics Award and a People's Choice Award for that role. Next came Jonathan Lynn's *Clue*, then *Choose Me*, and *Songwriter* (for which she received a Best Actress Golden Globe nomination). Other feature credits include *Cop* with James Woods, Mel Brooks's *Life Stinks*, *Pure Country*, the independent feature film production *Bird of Prey*, and the controversial, erotic thriller *Color of Night*.

There are two scenes from *Splendor in the Grass* that had a lasting effect on me. There's a scene where Natalie Wood is confronted by her mother that is very fresh in my memory. She's in the bathtub, and her mother is questioning her about being a "good girl." She's caught between what I felt was the quintessential struggle between those two generations: A "good girl" did not have sexual feelings and never ever was supposed to act on them if she did have them. That scene epitomized Deanie's struggle to please her mother. Metaphorically, it's about trying to please society in general. Rather than disappointing her mother or forming a separate identity, she became emotionally paralyzed, couldn't make a decision about who she was and what she wanted. Because Deanie was unable to extricate herself from that kind of pressure—her mother was so suffocating—she turned on herself in rage and frustration, with a kind of hysteria that led to an ultimate breakdown.

I grew up in the generation right after that, and it was still a struggle. I grew up thinking you had to be a virgin until you married. It was a struggle that

Natalie Wood in *Splendor in the Grass*, 1961

"Don't you have any shame?" She becomes hysterical and starts crying, speaking in an incoherent manner, saying that she has no shame. The reality is that she couldn't be like the tough girls. She's not the good girl that her mother thinks she is; she has no definition of her own. Her identity has always been defined by her mother, by society, and now, by men. She goes through a long and arduous process, with a lot of pain, where she is finally able to extricate herself from the morals of the time. Finally, at the end of the movie, she becomes her own woman.

This movie just had an amazing impact on me. I know so many women, so many girls at that age, and so many girls today, who experience that kind of flip-flopping between wanting to please their mother or father and defining themselves through men. Ultimately, they have to work through all of that to find themselves.

I first saw *Splendor in the Grass* in New York when I was about thirteen. Actually, I think I saw it with my mother. We used to go to movies a lot together. I think I saw it again when I was on location somewhere. It was on TV, and I watched it, and I went right back to remembering the awful sort of yearning and upset feeling I had when I first watched it. There is always this split in women. It's the classic Madonna/Whore split: Whom do you serve? How do you ultimately get to know who you are and separate it from these role models that are forced upon you? Even today when I do a movie or a scene that might have some sexuality to it, I feel nervous about telling my mother. ✪

women consistently had. Even today they have it, although there are more subtle terms to grapple with.

The other scene from *Splendor in the Grass* that had a lasting effect on me was the one where Deanie has a wild, emotional pendulum swing. It's a reaction to what happened between her and her mother. She cuts her hair off, puts on a lot of make-up, and starts to put on a tough veneer, trying to emulate those so-called "bad girls," who get the guys.

She has a scene where she is trying to seduce Warren Beatty's character. He is sick with a kind of sadness about what she has turned herself into. He pleads with her to stop. He says something like,

gene**Wilder**

the circus

Gene Wilder, born Jerry Silberman in Milwaukee, Wisconsin, achieved a reputation as one of the funniest and most inventive movie actors as early as 1967 when he won a Best Supporting Actor Oscar nomination for his performance in Mel Brooks's *The Producers*. Earlier that year, Wilder had made his motion picture debut in the small but memorable role of a nervous undertaker in *Bonnie and Clyde*. Since then, he has appeared in off-beat roles in *Quackser Fortune Has a Cousin in the Bronx*, *Willie Wonka and the Chocolate Factory*, Woody Allen's *Everything You Always Wanted to Know About Sex*, and as part of Brooks's celebrated "stock company" for a series of outrageously satirical films, *Blazing Saddles*, *The Frisco Kid*, and *The Woman in Red*, among others.

With Brooks's *Young Frankenstein* in 1974, Wilder not only starrred but made his screenwriting debut, earning a second Oscar nomination. He made his directorial bow the following year with *The Adventures of Sherlock Holmes' Smarter Brother*, in which he also played the title role from his own screenplay. Wilder's collaborations with comedian Richard Pryor have also been highly successful, beginning with their first pairing in *Silver Streak*, followed by *Stir Crazy*; *See No Evil, Hear No Evil*; and *Another You*.

If, as a youngster, I would have known to pay more attention to Bob Hope than I did to Errol Flynn, I think I would have been more consistently funny in my film career. I swayed, like a drunken sailor, between wanting to make people laugh and wanting to be seen as a romantic hero.

My home life, of course, had so much to do with this. Still, when a boy or girl is struggling to define what's going on inside, the characters we see on screen can make us say, "that's who I am."

Fortunately, after growing out of *Zorro*, I was scared to death by the Frankenstein monster, and those fears (and wanting to rewrite the endings) lasted, subliminally, into my adult career.

And then I saw Chaplin in *City Lights*. I was seventeen.

There he was, romancing a blind girl, trying to be charming and serious as he held a ball of yarn between his hands for her. And then he realizes that she has caught a thread of his long underwear on her needles and is slowly undressing him.

In another scene from *City Lights*, Charlie is drunk and trying to eat his spaghetti, but his fork gets caught on one of the New Year's Eve decorations, so instead of spaghetti he eats a mile-long paper streamer.

In *The Circus*, Charlie is starving and sees a little boy eating a long hotdog while his father holds him. Charlie takes a quick bite of hotdog whenever the father turns away; when the father turns back, Charlie pretends he is playing with the little boy.

I think it was after seeing that particular scene from *The Circus* that this great epiphany hit me in the head and in the heart: You don't have to choose between the clown and the sensitive hero.

A conscious way of working began to form. Not to imitate Chaplin (God forbid), but to find a truly funny physical task that has psychological implications, and then perform it as truthfully as possible without trying to "act" funny.

I'm not a comedian, so the lesson of Chaplin for me (apart from the genius of his performance) was the answer to an actor's quest: If you want to be funny, trust in behavior and don't worry about being funny.

When I succeed, I am funny; when I fail, I think it's because somewhere inside I'm still trying to be Errol Flynn or Leslie Howard. ✪

Merna Kennedy and Charles Chaplin in *The Circus*, 1928

ziegfeld girl

esther **Williams**

Esther Williams swam her way to stardom in such pictures as *Bathing Beauty, Ziegfeld Follies, Neptune's Daughter, Million Dollar Mermaid,* and *Dangerous When Wet*—swimming more than 1,250 miles in twenty-five aquamusicals for MGM.

As a competitor, Williams won three berths on the U.S. Olympic team headed for Helsinki, Finland, in 1940; however, World War II broke out, and the games were canceled. MGM executives spotted her as Olympic champion Johnny Weismuller's co-star in Billy Rose's San Francisco Aquacade. She made her screen debut alongside Mickey Rooney in *Andy Hardy's Double Life,* giving the popular hero his first kiss—underwater. The personification of synchronized swimming and graceful water ballet, Williams remains America's favorite swimming star.

My favorite movie moment is not only a favorite moment, but it became a turning point in my life. I've thought about it many times when I was making movies. It's a moment from *Ziegfeld Girl*, and I'm going to describe the impact it had on me by relating something from that period in my life.

When I was eighteen, I was starring in Billy Rose's Aquacade at the San Francisco Fair of 1940. I was so naive. It was the first time I was away from home, and I was the victim of what you'd call today sexual harassment. I needed somebody to turn to, so I married a young medical student at USC, whose parents ran out of money for his education. We eloped, and I moved to Los Angeles and supported him while he was going to medical school.

I came down to Los Angeles from the Aquacade, and even though MGM had spotted me up there and sent a very famous agent from the William Morris office by the name of Johnny Hyde to ask me to do a screen test, I said no. From what I'd seen at the Aquacade—there was a lot of promiscuity going on—show business looked like a very bad way to go. All I wanted to do was to get out of that carnival atmosphere. Billy Rose was very cheap, I had a terrible little dressing room with a cracked mirror, and

Hedy Lamarr, Tony Martin, and Lana Turner in *Ziegfeld Girl*, 1941

of executives, and a top agent, well, they just have to have you. Saying no to L. B. Mayer? They had never heard of such a thing.

What I didn't know at the time was that MGM had looked at the Sonja Henie ice-skating pictures, and they thought, "Why don't we melt the ice and put somebody in the water? Make it a swimming thing, with pretty girls in bathing suits."

So Johnny Hyde was given the job of calling me all the time. I kept saying no, and the sales girls, who were all my friends, nearly went crazy. "Just go meet L. B. Mayer. If nothing else, it's something you can tell your grandchildren." They were constantly at me. Finally, one hot August day—something had happened to the air conditioning in the store, and everybody was in kind of a blue mood—Johnny Hyde called. He said, "I'm tired of calling." (It had been a whole year now.) "I'm sending a limousine, and I'm going to be in the back seat." He said we were going to MGM, and I was going to meet Mr. Mayer. So, the girls dressed me in I. Magnin clothes, because I had no real clothes. The buyer happened to be off that day or we would never have gotten away with it. They dressed me in this beautiful I. Magnin wardrobe, but they warned me to be back by six o'clock, because that's when the store closes. It was really *Cinderella*.

The limo arrived, and there sat tiny Johnny Hyde. He was small enough to be a jockey, sitting in the back seat in this great big limo. I said to him as I got into the car, "One thing we're not going to do is walk in together. You're going in ahead, and you sit down, and then I will come in." I was a model and knew how to walk. "You will make me look nine feet tall."

there were about two inches of water in it all the time. So when they came up and said to me, "You're gonna be a movie star," I said, "No, I'm not. Are you crazy? You people are all nuts." They said MGM is a very beautiful place, and why don't you just table your thinking until you see it.

To put Leonard through medical school I was modeling at I. Magnin, and I was also hanging stock, making all of $78 a month. While I was working at the department store—I worked on the sportswear floor, and they let me wear the clothes—Johnny Hyde had been given an order to sign me. Somehow the word "no" is very magical, especially in the movie business. If you say no to L. B. Mayer, and his whole third floor

I went in, and I did walk the long walk. L. B. Mayer had an office with a long approach to his desk, and he could look you over very carefully by the time you arrived at his white leather, crescent-shaped desk. The entire third floor of MGM executives was seated there in his office. When I got to the end of that walk, L. B. Mayer said, "My God, you're tall."

I looked at Johnny Hyde, and I said, "I told you I was too tall. You dragged me out of the store, and I have to get back at six o'clock. I don't thank you for this, Mr. Hyde."

I turned on my heel and walked back on that long walk out. L. B. Mayer called out, "Come back and sit down. You're not *that* tall. Ingrid Bergman is taller than you, and she works with Charles Boyer and Humphrey Bogart, so come back!"

So I went back and sat down. They told me what it would be like, and I told them what my fears were. I said, I don't belong here. They showed me a dressing room, and it was wonderful. It was bigger than where I lived. I looked at the studio and saw these wonderful stars walking around, and I thought, "I don't belong here. I'm not trained. I've never acted. I've never even asked anybody for an autograph."

My only experience with movies was that I went to the Saturday matinees and saw movies once in a while, but the only one that had made any impact on me was *Gone With the Wind* because I liked Clark Gable so much. I had never done drama. The only drama-related thing that I had done was to write the football skits for my high school pep rallies. I never even thought of being in them. I never considered performing. I thought that would be kind of dumb. I was a swimmer. Then, the strangest thing happened.

That night, my husband and I went to see *Ziegfeld Girl*. The entire film was so beautifully mounted, and when Tony Martin sang "You Stepped Out of a Dream," and Lana Turner, Hedy Lamarr, and Judy Garland walked down those stairs, I thought, "I want to be in the movies." When I saw those beautiful clothes and that beautiful production—and with Tony Martin singing that song as the women walked down the stairway—I knew it was for me.

When we got home, I told my husband that I wanted to be in movies. He said, "If you go to that studio and sign a contract, that's the end of us." (It really was a turning point. We really didn't belong together, after all.)

The next day, I put on my own clothes, and called a taxi. (I didn't even know how to drive.) I told Johnny Hyde that I was going to the studio and that I would meet him there. I said, "I want to sign a contract."

Then something happened that reaffirmed what my mother always said to me: All things work together for good. It turned out my screen test was with Clark Gable. Lana Turner, who was to star with Gable in *Somewhere I'll Find You*, had gone off and married Artie Shaw, and L. B. Mayer was mad at her. So he decided to replace her with a newcomer. I did the test with Gable, and the craziest thing was I got the part.

That scene where Tony Martin sang "You Stepped Out of a Dream" changed my life, and, now, whenever I see Tony, he sings it to me. ✪

gone with the wind

jobeth**Williams**

JoBeth Williams made her screen debut in *Kramer vs. Kramer* as Dustin Hoffman's overnight guest, who suffers an embarrassing introduction to his son. A graduate of Brown University with a major in English, Williams joined the prestigious Trinity Repertory Theatre in Rhode Island soon after receiving her diploma. Making her New York stage debut in the off-Broadway production of Michael Weller's *Moonchildren*, she continued to accumulate notable theater credits.

Following her role in *Kramer vs. Kramer*, Williams was cast in *Stir Crazy* and *The Dogs of War*. Steven Spielberg subsequently cast her in her first leading role—the terrified housewife in *Poltergeist*, and she went on to star in numerous films, including *Poltergeist II: The Other Side*, *The Big Chill*, *Teachers*, *American Dreamer*, *Memories of Me*, *Dutch*, *Switch*, *Stop! Or My Mom Will Shoot*, and the epic saga *Wyatt Earp*.

She directed 1994's *On Hope*, nominated for a Best Achievement in Live Action Short Films Academy Award.

Vivien Leigh in *Gone With the Wind*, 1939

The scene that's affected me the most was from *Gone With the Wind*. It was the power of Scarlett. Before I saw that movie I had never seen a female character like her. As a child, I wanted to *be* her. And I *was* for quite a while: I used to flounce around the house in my mother's petticoats.

Scarlett's spirit really struck me, inspired me. The moment I remember most is the silhouette of her against Tara, with that wonderful sky and that lone tree. That image has always stayed with me. Her spirit, that she never give up Tara, and the overall beauty of the film made a lasting impression on me.

I've always been very attracted to spunky female characters, many of Katharine Hepburn's roles, for instance. Even as a kid, I was drawn to those kinds of films, those with a strong woman character. They did something to me. That silhouette of Scarlett standing there alone with Tara in the background has always stayed with me. ✪

Jeffrey Hunter, John Wayne, and Ward Bond in *The Searchers*, 1956

irwin**Winkler**

the searchers

Irwin Winkler commands a distinguished reputation in the motion picture industry as one of its most progressive and honored filmmakers. His films have received twelve Academy Awards out of forty-five nominations, including four Best Picture nominations—a record that stands alone in contemporary Hollywood.

Winkler started his producing career at MGM with the Elvis Presley movie *Double Trouble*. He and long-time associate Robert Chartoff mortgaged their homes to finance their Sylvester Stallone vehicle, *Rocky*. The film earned the Academy Award for Best Picture in 1976. Winkler's other Best Picture nominations were for *Raging Bull*, *The Right Stuff*, and *Goodfellas*, while *They Shoot Horses, Don't They?* amassed nine Oscar nominations.

Winkler and Chartoff followed their debut with the Lee Marvin thriller *Point Blank*, now considered a cult classic. They went on to produce the multi-nominated *They Shoot Horses, Don't They?*, *Leo the Last*, and *The Strawberry Statement*. Winkler began his long relationship with director Martin Scorsese by producing *New York, New York*, followed by *Raging Bull*.

In 1989, Winkler made his directorial debut with *Guilty By Suspicion*. Next came *Night and the City* and *Music Box*. *Goodfellas*, Winkler's third project with Scorsese as director, was 1990's winner of both the New York Film Critics' and the L.A. Film Critics' Awards for Best Film, the British Academy Awards Best Picture, as well as numerous other honors.

My favorite moment is from *The Searchers*, John Ford's movie in which John Wayne's family is massacred by Indians, except for a young girl, who is captured by them. Wayne and two other men go out to find her.

The moment comes as the three men are on the trail. They reach a pass, and Wayne tells the other two guys to ride around it, while he rides through. Then Ford cuts to the two fellows waiting on the other side of the pass, waiting for Wayne. Finally, he comes riding in, very distraught, and they say to him, "We think we saw her." She was wearing the dress that they had captured her in.

Wayne, very angrily, says something like, "That's not her."

He says that's just an Indian girl wearing the dress. "I saw her back in the pass, and she's dead," he replies.

They ask him what the Indians did to her. Wayne says, "As long as you live, never ask me to tell you about what they did to her."

That's the most violent moment I've ever seen in film, because the mind conjures up what they did to her. You never see a thing. The brilliance of Ford was heightening violence by not showing it. To me, that's a seminal moment in filmmaking. I first saw it on television, probably thirty years ago, and I've seen that film fifteen or twenty times since. I always marvel at that particular moment. ✪

robert Wise

the ten commandments

Robert Wise was introduced to film at dime matinees in his rural hometown, and later became a messenger in the editing department of RKO. He advanced rapidly, becoming a full editor in 1939, assigned to work with such directors as William Dieterle, Garson Kanin, Orson Welles, and Val Lewton. Wise earned an Academy Award nomination as editor of *Citizen Kane* (1941) and also edited and supervised the revisions to Welles's second film classic, *The Magnificent Ambersons* (1942). Lewton promoted Wise from editor to director midway through production of *Curse of the Cat People* (1944). After carving a new career out of "B" movie directorial assignments, Wise directed his first "A" picture, the western *Blood on the Moon* (1948). With his next assignment, *The Set-Up* (1949), Wise won the Critics Prize at Cannes.

Wise left RKO, turning out a succession of solid films, including *The Day the Earth Stood Still* (1951), *Executive Suite* (1954), *Somebody Up There Likes Me* (1956), *Run Silent, Run Deep* (1958), *I Want to Live!* (1958), and *Odds Against Tomorrow* (1959). In the 1960s, his blockbusters *West Side Story* (1961) and *The Sound of Music* (1965) each earned him double Oscars as Best Director (with co-director Jerome Robbins on *West Side*) and producer of the year's Best Picture. Wise has been responsible for other popular films, including *The Haunting* (1963), *The Sand Pebbles* (1966), *The Andromeda Strain* (1971), *The Hindenburg* (1975), and *Star Trek: The Motion Picture* (1979).

I grew up in Indiana, in Cartersville, a town of about 12,000. We had three movie houses there, a very small one, a medium-sized one, and the biggest one, the Auditorium. It was a good-sized house, probably 600 to 700 seats. It had a balcony in addition to the main floor, and it had an orchestra pit.

This was in the days of vaudeville. On weekends we used to have vaudeville acts that came in. The big event was a road show picture, a DeMille picture, *The Ten Commandments*—that was the big event of that particular season. When we saw the announcement that it was coming, three or four months ahead, we just couldn't wait. They did the things we later did with *The Sound of Music* and *West Side Story*. You got your tickets in advance. You had reserved seats. It was a major event. There was a twenty-five- or thirty-piece orchestra in the pit, and before the show they played the orchestral score of *The Ten Commandments*.

That's a very civilized way to see films. That has always been one of my outstanding memories of my early, early falling in love with the movies. That's when I knew I was really hooked. ✪

the red balloon

alfre**Woodard**

Alfre Woodard made her motion picture debut in Alan Rudolph's *Remember My Name*, and in 1984 earned an Academy Award nomination for her performance in Martin Ritt's *Cross Creek*. She has appeared in John Sayles's *Passion Fish*, Bruce Beresford's *Rich in Love*, William Friedkin's *Blue Chips*, and the comedy *Heart and Souls*, as well as Lawrence Kasdan's *Grand Canyon*, Spike Lee's *Crooklyn*, and the film adaptation of the novel *How to Make an American Quilt*. She starred opposite Danny Glover in director Morgan Freeman's compelling South African drama *Bopha!*

A two-time Emmy Award winner, Woodard was first honored in 1984 for a performance on the series *Hill Street Blues*, and won her second Emmy for a role on the pilot of *L.A. Law*. Always drawn to the theater, Woodard numbers among her stage credits the New York Shakespeare Festival production of David Hare's *Map of the World* in 1985, and the 1989 production of *A Winter's Tale*.

Pascal Lamorisse in *The Red Balloon*, 1955

Somebody was always taking me to the movies. In my youth, my viewing fare was determined by my six- and four-year-old sister and brother, who decreed that Disney was definitely not an option and that terror was entertainment. And, of course, entertainment was the only conceivable reason to sit through a movie. Footloose, privileged Negro children at the colored movie house: Milk Duds and horror. Images from *The Pit and the Pendulum*, *The Creature from the Black Lagoon*, and *The Untouchables* mauraded my sweet, nappy head at night.

At fourteen, it was an excitable Brother Patrick O'Brien hurrying me into my seat at the Southroads Cinema to view yet another one of his monthly all-Bishop Kelley High School screenings. Sometimes I even had to read while watching a movie, depending on the country of origin, but at least Orson Welles's massive head looming in my dreams didn't make me throw up. *Sundays and Cybele*, *Citizen Kane*, *Incident at Owl Creek*, et al. required written dramatic criticism from every pupil, grades nine through twelve, and I was game for analyzing. I was pleased to have something to argue besides what color I thought "The Thing's" puke would be. My thinking was elevated to an awareness of movies as a craft.

But I was still being taken to the movies. A smiling bystander. An easy date. Until the afternoon I sat in the dark with Brother Pat and his seven hundred charges to watch Albert Lamouisse's *The Red Balloon*.

It could have been my very first movie. I was transported. It was the most perfectly simple and clearest story that had ever been told to me on film. A film with no dialogue! I was captivated. I realized the real story, as in life, lies somewhere between the lines. As I watched young Pascal maneuver the streets of 1950-something Paris, teasing and toying with a provocative red balloon, I realized an object could be a character. I was delighted. And his red balloon showed me more about loyalty and the triumph of the heart than the far more ambitious and grandiose tales told to me for that purpose. I was strengthened. I realized at the end credits that I had understood every gesture, every intention.

And the entire film was in silent French. I was tickled.

I got it! Movies are stories. (The good ones still are.) Like my Mama and my Uncle Walter and my Daddy and my everybody used to tell and retell and pass on with their personal topspin. I was connected. *The Red Balloon* connected me to film for the first time. I saw the possibilities. They were suddenly accessible to me. No one would ever "take" me to the movies again. I was an active participant. ✪

Pascal Lamorisse in *The Red Balloon*, 1955

butch cassidy and the sundance kid

lilifini Zanuck

Oscar-winning producer Lili Fini Zanuck began her career as a production coordinator at the Zanuck Brown Co., and after two years of hands-on production work, discovered and optioned the unpublished science-fiction manuscript for *Cocoon*. The 1985 project, co-produced by Zanuck, went on to win two Academy Awards and was followed by *Cocoon: The Return*.

In 1988, she and husband Richard Zanuck formed the Zanuck Company. The company's first endeavor, and Zanuck's third effort, 1989's *Driving Miss Daisy*, garnered four Oscars—including Best Picture of the Year—a Golden Globe Award, and earned Zanuck a Producer of the Year honor from the Producers Guild of America. Her other producing credits include *Rich in Love, Clean Slate, Wild Bill, Mulholland Falls*, and the thriller *The Day After Tomorrow*.

Zanuck made her directorial debut with *Rush* in 1992 and has directed *The Double* and *Sequestered Jury*, which she also co-produced.

t

This is extremely politically incorrect. It's an impression that has stayed with me since I was very young. It's from when I saw *Butch Cassidy and the Sundance Kid* for the very first time. It's the scene where Katharine Ross comes home, and Robert Redford is sitting in a chair with a gun. He tells her to get undressed. I was about fourteen at the time, a Catholic girl who went to Confession every Friday. As I sat in the theater watching that scene, I saw it as the answer to all of my problems. I could picture myself going to Confession and telling the priest that Robert Redford came into my room with a gun and made me get undressed.

I was impressed by it because it had a kind of romantic quality about it. At first, you didn't know that they knew each other. You thought he was an

182

intruder. It had a little bit of danger, and it was a very sexy scene to me at that age. It always stayed in my mind as just about the best thing that could happen to you: You'd come home, and Robert Redford would be in a chair with a gun and make you get undressed. The only thing that could top that is if he paid you a million dollars to do it. ✪

Katharine Ross in *Butch Cassidy and the Sundance Kid*, 1969

robert**Z**emeckis

bonnie and clyde

Director Robert Zemeckis is the creative talent behind some of the most popular films in motion picture history, ranging from *Romancing the Stone* and the *Back to the Future* trilogy to his record-breaking blockbuster *Forrest Gump*, for which Zemeckis was awarded the 1994 Best Director Golden Globe, named Best Director of the year by the Directors Guild of America, and received the Academy Award for Best Director.

Zemeckis made his feature directing debut in 1978 with *I Wanna Hold Your Hand*, a nostalgic comedy about a group of teenagers who try to meet the Beatles on the eve of their first appearance on *The Ed Sullivan Show*. He and his longtime writing partner, Bob Gale, co-wrote the film, which Steven Spielberg executive produced. They followed up this success with the innovative comedies *1941* and *Used Cars*. *Romancing the Stone* (1984) came next and, the following year, Zemeckis directed the Zemeckis-Gale screenplay, *Back to the Future*, which inspired two sequels. For his next feature, *Who Framed Roger Rabbit?* (1988), Zemeckis spent two years perfecting the process of directing live actors opposite animated "toons." Zemeckis also directed the 1992 dark comedy *Death Becomes Her*, and executive produced two 1992 releases, *The Public Eye*, and the action-thriller *Trespass*, which he co-wrote with Gale.

My most memorable movie moment comes from the time I saw *Bonnie and Clyde* for the first time. I saw it in Chicago, when I was growing up. I loved to go to the movies, particularly action movies and those with special effects, where I'd ask the question, "How did they do that?"

There's a scene in the movie where Gene Hackman has been shot in the head, and he's dying. The Barrow Gang had been ambushed the night before in a motor court, and Gene Hackman had been badly wounded. They had made their getaway and slept all night in their cars in this field. In the morning, just as they're getting up, they were surrounded on all sides by lawmen, who started blazing away.

Because he's got his head all bandaged up and is in very bad condition, Hackman just stumbles around and is not able to escape. We actually watch him die right in front of us. His right hand twitches at the end.

Estelle Parsons and Gene Hackman in *Bonnie and Clyde*, 1967

I remember being so moved by that. I think I was in junior high school at the time, and that was the first moment where I was moved emotionally by a movie. I thought, "Boy, I've got to check into this. Something really powerful is going on here."

Seeing that scene is when my interest in film shifted 180 degrees from my just being fascinated with technique to understanding the true power of the motion-picture story. What movies do is move you emotionally, and everything else is there to serve that. That image of Gene Hackman dying in the field is still a very, very strong image in my mind. That's probably the day that I decided to become a movie director. ✪

the creators of
private screenings

The American Film Institute is the nation's most distinguished and highly respected guardian of our film heritage. A non-profit organization, AFI is dedicated to the study of all aspects of the art and industry of film making as well as to the restoration and preservation of classic movies.

Duane Byrge is the senior film critic for *The Hollywood Reporter* and an adjunct faculty member of the American Film Institute, where he moderates the Directors on Directing course. He holds a Ph.D. in Communications, with an emphasis in Cinema, from the University of Southern California and has served as lecturer there. Byrge has written for television, and his Ph.D. dissertation was the basis for the book *The Screwball Comedy Films*, which he co-authored.

acknowledgments

The goals of The American Film Institute would never be fully realized without the help of friends from around the world.

First, a special thanks to you, the reader for supporting the work of AFI through the purchase of *Private Screenings*. Your enjoyment of the special movie moments in this book will benefit AFI's efforts to illuminate America's film and television past, to empower image makers for the future, and to honor the art of the moving image.

Others to whom we extend our gratitude:

To the film artists who shared their favorite movie memories with us. The response was so overwhelming that printing all of them would have produced a book the size of *Gone With the Wind*. Unfortunately, this means that included in these pages is a sincere thanks to the friends whose submissions we were not able to include.

To the good people of Turner Publishing, who had to make the painful cuts, and who guided us through this project with patience and professionalism.

To Duane Byrge—friend and colleague to AFI—whose interviews served as a catalyst for many of these wonderful memories.

And last, but certainly not least, to the team at AFI who worked to produce a book worthy of its topic: Bob Gazzale, Lillian Dean, Mimi Korpics, and Maggie Biggar. We are proud of these members of the AFI work family.

If you wish to become a member or receive more information about The American Film Institute, please call: 1-800-774-4AFI.

Jean Firstenberg
Director—The American Film Institute

James Hindman
Deputy Director—The American Film Institute

187

photo credits

The movie stills included in this book are courtesy of the following:

ABC/Viacom: *Duel in the Sun; The Magic Box.* **Bubbles Inc.:** *The Circus; City Lights; The Gold Rush; The Kid; Modern Times.* **Columbia Pictures:** *Born Yesterday; 8½; Glory; The Graduate; Guess Who's Coming to Dinner; Lawrence of Arabia; Picnic.* **The Disney Company:** *Treasure Island.* **Janus:** *Great Expectations; Rashomon; The Red Balloon; Red Beard; The Seven Samurai; The Third Man; White Mane.* **MCA Universal:** *The Deer Hunter; The Mummy; The Ten Commandments.* **MGM/UA:** *Apocalypse Now; In the Heat of the Night ; Lilies of the Field; Last Tango in Paris; Muriel; What's New, Pussycat?* **Paramount:** *The Apprenticeship of Duddy Kravitz; Don't Look Now; The Education of Sonny Carson; The Godfather; The Lady Eve.* **Photofest:** *Ashes and Diamonds; The Deer Hunter; Glory.* **Republic Entertainment:** *It's a Wonderful Life; Long Day's Journey Into Night.* **Rhi Entertainment:** *The Keystone Cops.* **Samuel Goldwyn:** *The Pride of the Yankees; Wuthering Heights.* **Turner Entertainment Company:** *The Battle of the Century; Bringing Up Baby; Captains Courageous; Citizen Kane; Dr. Zhivago; Gone With the Wind; The Good Earth; Gunga Din; The Informer; Little Caesar; Romance; The Treasure of the Sierra Madre; 2001: A Space Odyssey; Yankee Doodle Dandy; Ziegfeld Girl.* **Twentieth Century Fox:** *All About Eve; A Man Called Peter; The Ox-Bow Incident; State Fair; A Tree Grows in Brooklyn; Butch Cassidy and the Sundance Kid.* **Warner Bros.:** *Bonnie and Clyde; Day for Night; Indiscreet; My Fair Lady; Rebel Without a Cause; The Searchers; Splendor in the Grass; Unforgiven.* **Zaentz Company:** *One Flew Over the Cuckoo's Nest.*

Contributor portrait credits:

Keith Carradine photo by Jeff Sedlik; Martha Coolidge photo by Jane O'Neal; Roger Ebert photo by Tom Maday; William Friedkin photo by Bob Greene; Scott Glenn photo by Peter Kredenser; Randa Haines photo by Robert Zuckerman; Charlton Heston photo by Lee Salem; Ron Howard photo by Ron Batzdorff; Lawrence Kasdan photo by Etienne George; George Lucas photo by Minisei Toinaga; Gordon Parks photo by Abe Frajndlich; Daniel Petrie photo by Hella Hammid; Robert Redford photo by Jean Pagliuso; Martin Scorsese photo by Patrick Demarchelier; Ron Shelton photo by Sidney Baldwin; John Singleton photo by Anthony Barboza; Steven Spielberg photo by Murray Close; Wayne Wang photo by Lorey Sebastin; Lesley Ann Warren photo by Paul Jasmine; Irwin Winkler photo by Phillip Saltonstall; Robert Zemeckis photo by Dana Gluckstein.